A Note From Rick Renner

I am on a personal quest to see a "revival of the Bible" so people can establish their lives on a firm foundation that will stand strong and endure the test as end-time storm winds begin to intensify.

In order to experience a revival of the Bible in your personal life, it is important to take time each day to read, receive, and apply its truths to your life. James tells us that if we will continue in the perfect law of liberty — refusing to be forgetful hearers, but determined to be doers — we will be blessed in our ways. As you watch or listen to the programs in this series and work through this corresponding study guide, I trust you will search the Scriptures and allow the Holy Spirit to help you hear something new from God's Word that applies specifically to your life. I encourage you to be a doer of the Word He reveals to you. Whatever the cost, I assure you — it will be worth it.

> Thy words were found, and I did eat them;
> and thy word was unto me the joy and rejoicing of mine heart:
> for I am called by thy name, O Lord God of hosts.
> — Jeremiah 15:16

Your brother and friend in Jesus Christ,

Rick Renner

How To Use This Study Guide

This five-lesson study guide corresponds to *"Demas and Deception" With Rick Renner* (Renner TV). Each lesson in this study guide covers a topic that is addressed during the program series, with questions and references supplied to draw you deeper into your own private study of the Scriptures on this subject.

To derive the most benefit from this study guide, consider the following:

First, watch or listen to the program prior to working through the corresponding lesson in this guide. (Programs can also be viewed at **renner.org** by clicking on the Media/Archives links or on our Renner Ministries YouTube channel.)

Second, take the time to look up the scriptures included in each lesson. Prayerfully consider their application to your own life.

Third, use a journal or notebook to make note of your answers to each lesson's Study Questions and Practical Application challenges.

Fourth, invest specific time in prayer and in the Word of God to consult with the Holy Spirit. Write down the scriptures or insights He reveals to you.

Finally, take action! Whatever the Lord tells you to do according to His Word, do it.

For added insights on this subject, it is recommended that you obtain Rick Renner's books *How To Keep Your Head on Straight in a World Gone Crazy: Developing Discernment for These Last Days*. You may also select from Rick's other available resources by placing your order at **renner.org** or by calling 1-800-742-5593.

TOPIC

Who Was Demas and Why Did He Abandon His Faith?

SCRIPTURES

1. **Mark 4:3,4** — Hearken; Behold, there went out a sower to sow: And it came to pass, as he sowed, some fell by the way side, and the fowls of the air came and devoured it up.

2. **Mark 4:15** — And these are they by the way side, where the word is sown; but when they have heard, Satan cometh immediately, and taketh away the word that was sown in their hearts.

3. **Mark 4:5,6** — And some fell on stony ground, where it had not much earth; and immediately it sprang up, because it had no depth of earth: But when the sun was up, it was scorched; and because it had no root, it withered away.

4. **Mark 4:16,17** — And these are they likewise which are sown on stony ground; who, when they have heard the word, immediately receive it with gladness; and have no root in themselves, and so endure but for a time: afterward, when affliction or persecution ariseth for the word's sake, immediately they are offended.

5. **Mark 4:7** — And some fell among thorns, and the thorns grew up, and choked it, and it yielded no fruit.

6. **Mark 4:18,19** — And these are they which are sown among thorns; such as hear the word, and the cares of this world, and the deceit-fulness of riches, and the lusts of other things entering in, choke the word, and it becometh unfruitful.

7. **Mark 4:8** — And other fell on good ground, and did yield fruit that sprang up and increased; and brought forth, some thirty, and some sixty, and some an hundred

8. **Colossians 4:14** — Luke, the beloved physician, and Demas, greet you.

9. **Philemon 1:23,24** — There salute thee Epaphras, my fellowprisoner in Christ Jesus; Marcus [Mark], Aristarchus, Demas, Lucas [Luke], my fellowlabourers.

10. **2 Timothy 4:9,10** — Do thy diligence to come shortly unto me: For Demas hath forsaken me, having loved this present world, and is departed unto Thessalonica....

GREEK WORDS

1. "Luke" — Λουκᾶς (*Loukas*): a Christian physician, and writer of the gospel of Luke and the book of Acts; traveling companion and fellow prisoner of the apostle Paul

2. "beloved" — ἀγαπητός (*agapetos*): loved, beloved, or deeply cherished; derived from ἀγάπη (*agape*), a word that describes one's deep love for someone else, and hence, one who is beloved; the word ἀγάπη (*agape*) describes the admiration one had for an object of beauty; the onlooker was so taken by the object that it caused a deep admiration and appreciation to come out of his heart because he was so moved by what he has beheld; here, the word ἀγαπητός (*agapetos*) describes the deep admiration, affection, awe, and wonder that people felt for Luke and Demas

3. "and" — καί (*kai*): and, also, even, or indeed

4. "Demas" — Δημᾶς (Demas): a companion and helper of the apostle Paul; here, spoken of with commendation as one in whom the apostle had confidence; some scholars believe that Demas was the one who actually penned the book of Colossians as it was dictated by Paul; he was likely from aristocracy, privilege, and wealth

5. "greet" — ἀσπάζομαι (*aspadzomai*): to pay respect to, salute, or to warmly greet and welcome; used as a high greeting for distinguished persons, and it was also used for soldiers who saluted fellow soldiers; the root means to draw near, as to pull another person to oneself; an endearing term intended to communicate camaraderie, dearness, and warmth; because it was used as a greeting for distinguished persons or as a salute to soldiers, it means Luke and Demas were acknowledging the believers they were addressing were faithful, fellow soldiers in battle, whom they wished to salute

6. "Epaphras" — Ἐπαφρᾶς (*Epaphras*): leader of the Colossian church who was sent by the church to seek out and minister to Paul; possibly was cast into prison by Roman authorities on suspicion of being an accomplice of Paul

7. "fellowprisoner" — συναιχμάλωτος (*sunaichmalotos*): compound of the preposition σύν (*sun*) and αἰχμάλωτος (*aichmalotos*); the word

σύν (*sun*) means together and pictures partnership, and αἰχμάλωτος (*aichmalotos*) is a compound of αἰχμή (*aichme*), which pictures a spear, and ἁλωτός (*alotos*), which describes one taken captive at the point of a spear; as a compound, two who are together taken into captivity at the point of a spear; hence, forcibly taken captive as hostages in a war

8. "Mark" — Μάρκος (*Markos*): Mark, also called John Mark, who was the son of Mary, the nephew of Barnabas, and a fellow traveler in ministry with Barnabas, Paul, and Peter

9. "Aristarchus" — Ἀρίσταρχος (*Aristarchos*): literally, best-ruler; a Christian of Thessalonica and fellow prisoner with Paul; he was from aristocracy, privilege, and wealth

10. "fellowlaborers" — οἱ συνεργοί μου (*hoi sunergoi mou*): the plural form of συνεργός (*sunergos*) with a definite article and μου (*mou*); the word συνεργός (*sunergos*) is a compound of the preposition σύν (*sun*), which means together and pictures partnership, and the word ἔργον (*ergon*), which means work and pictures production; the word μου (*mou*) means of mine; used with the definite article οἱ (*hoi*), it means THE fellow workers of mine, stressing that these were the fellow team players who were associated with Paul; the word implies two people working closely together as partners sharing work and responsibility, and there is even the notion of equality in the word

11. "diligence" — σπουδάζω (*spoudadzo*): to do something with haste because it is so important, serious, or urgent; to give one's best efforts to a project or task and to do it enthusiastically

12. "shortly" — ταχέως (*tacheos*): from ταχύς (*tachus*); depicts a runner who runs as fast as he can; to move one's feet as fast as possible; to do something urgently; to do something as swiftly as possible

13. "forsaken" — ἐγκαταλείπω (*enkataleipo*): a compound of the prepositions ἐν (*en*) and κατά (*kata*), and the word λείπω (*leipo*); the preposition ἐν (*en*) means in, κατά (*kata*) means down, and the word λείπω (*leipo*) means to abandon, forsake, or leave behind; as a compound, to abandon, forsake, or leave in a bad situation; not only to desert, but to do it in the worst way and at the worst possible moment; not merely to leave, but to leave in the lurch

14. "having loved" — ἀγαπήσας (*agapesas*): from the word ἀγάπη (*agape*); describes the admiration one had for an object of beauty; the onlooker was so taken by the object that it caused a deep admiration and appreciation to come out of his heart because he was so moved by what he

had beheld; used in the New Testament to describe the love of God and one's love for God; here, however, Demas loved the world with a love that he should have only felt for God

15. "present world" — τὸν νῦν αἰῶνα (*ton nun aiona*): the definite article τὸν (*ton*) with νῦν (*nun*) and the word αἰῶνα (*aiona*); the word νῦν (*nun*) means right now or the present moment, and the word αἰῶνα (*aiona*) depicts an age with a concrete beginning and a concrete ending, or a measurable and limited age; as a phrase, the now age, this present age, or the here and now in this world

16. "departed" — πορεύομαι (*poreuomai*): here, pictures one who has departed or transitioned from a former position to another; the implication is Demas did not begin in a wrong place, but for some reason, he abandoned his former place or position to follow after a new place or position that was very different

SYNOPSIS

The five lessons in this study titled *Demas and Deception* will focus on the following topics:

- Who Was Demas and Why Did He Abandon His Faith?
- The Apostate Church at the End of the Age
- Resisting the Pressure To Accommodate the World
- Three Forces That Try To Lure You To Abandon Your Faith
- Concrete Steps To Be Sure You Never Become a Demas

The emphasis of this lesson:

Demas was a companion and deeply loved assistant to the apostle Paul. But somewhere along the way, the cares of this world, the deceitfulness of riches, and/or the lusts of other things choked out the truth of God's Word, and he abandoned his faith in Christ.

There is a person in the New Testament named Demas who helps us understand the dilemma of deception and why people fall away from the Lord. Maybe you know someone who has fallen away from the Lord. That is what happened to Demas, who was a companion and fellow traveler of the apostle Paul. A moment came when this well-trained and well-established minister deserted Paul and abandoned the faith. To understand what took place, we need to first examine Jesus' parable of the sower and the seed.

The Parable of the Sower and the Seed

In the parable of the sower, Jesus compares people with different types of soils. The "seed" being sown, or planted, is the Word of God, and the sower is the carrier of the Gospel. Jesus begins the telling of this story by saying, "Hearken; Behold, there went out a sower to sow: And it came to pass, as he sowed, some fell by the way side, and the fowls of the air came and devoured it up" (Mark 4:3,4).

The "seed sown by the way side" represents a certain group of people. Jesus Himself explains who they are by saying, "And these are they by the way side, where the word is sown; but when they have heard, Satan cometh immediately, and taketh away the word that was sown in their hearts" (Mark 4:15). So this category of people hears the Word, but immediately, Satan comes and attacks to steal the seed from their heart. As a result, they fall away.

A second group of people is described in Mark 4:5 and 6. Here, Jesus says, "And some fell on stony ground, where it had not much earth; and immediately it sprang up, because it had no depth of earth: But when the sun was up, it was scorched; and because it had no root, it withered away." Jesus clarifies who these individuals are in Mark 4:16 and 17, where He says, "And these are they likewise which are sown on stony ground; who, when they have heard the word, immediately receive it with gladness; and have no root in themselves, and so endure but for a time: afterward, when affliction or persecution ariseth for the word's sake, immediately they are offended."

The people described here are not really rooted and grounded in God's Word. This represents a significant number of people who, when opposition or persecution arises, get offended at people — or even at God — and fall away from the faith they once held dear.

A third category of people is described in Mark 4:7, where Jesus says, "And some fell among thorns, and the thorns grew up, and choked it, and it yielded no fruit." Like the first two groups, these individuals, as Jesus explained, were telling us, "they which are sown among thorns; such as hear the word, and the cares of this world, and the deceitfulness of riches, and the lusts of other things entering in, choke the word, and it becometh unfruitful" (Mark 4:18,19).

Again, these are people who hear God's Word, but in their case, things —
such as comfort, riches, possessions, and the potential loss of them — cause
these individuals to fall away. More than likely, it is this category of people
that Demas fell into. This brings us to the question of who is Demas and
why did he abandon his faith in Christ?

What the Bible Tells Us About Demas

The first mention of Demas in the New Testament is in Colossians 4:14,
where the apostle Paul writes, "Luke, the beloved physician, and Demas,
greet you." Clearly, Demas was a significant person, as Paul includes him
in the same closing greeting along with Luke. "Luke" — which in the
Greek is *Loukas* — was a Christian physician as well as the writer of the
gospel of Luke and the book of Acts. He was a traveling companion and
fellow prisoner of the apostle Paul.

Also notice the word "beloved," which describes not only Luke but also
Demas. It is a translation of the Greek word *agapetos*, which means *loved*,
beloved, or *deeply cherished*. It is derived from *agape*, a word that describes
one's deep love for someone else and, hence, *one who is beloved*. The word *agape*
describes *the admiration one has for an object of beauty*. The onlooker was so
taken by the object that it caused a deep admiration and appreciation to
come out of his heart because he was so moved by what he beheld.

In this verse, the word *agapetos* describes *the deep admiration, affection,
awe, and wonder that people felt for Luke and Demas*. We know it applies
to Demas as well because of the inclusion of the word "and," which is the
Greek word *kai*. It means *and, also, even*, or *indeed*. All that is said of Luke
also — or *even* and *indeed* — applies to Demas.

Demas was a companion and helper of the apostle Paul. Here in Colossians,
he is spoken of with commendation as one in whom the apostle Paul had
confidence. Interestingly, some scholars believe that Demas was the one who
actually penned the book of Colossians, as it was dictated by Paul, which
demonstrates just how close Demas and Paul were. More than likely, Demas
was from aristocracy, privilege, and wealth.

Again, as Paul was closing out his letter to the Colossians, he said that
Luke and Demas *greet you*. The word "greet" in Greek is *aspadzomai*, and
it means *to pay respect to, to salute*, or *to warmly greet and welcome*. It was
used as a high greeting for distinguished persons, and it was also used
for soldiers who saluted fellow soldiers. The root means *to draw near*, as

to pull another person to oneself. It is an endearing term intended to communicate camaraderie, dearness, and warmth. Because it was used as a greeting for distinguished persons or as a salute to soldiers, it indicates Luke and Demas were acknowledging the believers they were addressing were faithful, fellow soldiers in battle whom they wished to salute.

Demas Was a High-Level Christian Leader Who Served Alongside Other Like Leaders

The second mention of Demas is found in Paul's letter to Philemon. As he offered his closing remarks, he said, "There salute thee Epaphras, my fellowprisoner in Christ Jesus; Marcus [Mark], Aristarchus, Demas, Lucas [Luke], my fellowlabourers" (vv. 23,24). When we look closely at these two verses, it is surprising to see how much insight we can gather from them.

First, notice the name "Epaphras." He was the leader of the Colossian church who was sent to seek out and minister to Paul. It is very possible that Epaphras was cast into prison by Roman authorities on suspicion of being an accomplice of Paul's. This seems likely because Paul calls Epaphras his "fellowprisoner."

In Greek, the word "fellowprisoner" is *sunaichmalotos*, which is a compound of the preposition *sun* and *aichmalotos*. The word *sun* means *together* and pictures *partnership*; *aichmalotos* is a compound of *aichme*, which pictures *a spear*; and *alotos*, which describes *one taken captive at the point of a spear*. When these words are compounded to form *sunaichmalotos* — translated here as "fellowprisoner" — it describes *two who are together taken into captivity at the point of a spear*. Hence, they are forcibly taken captive as hostages in a war.

The next person Paul mentions as he closes his letter to Philemon is "Marcus," which in Greek is *Markos* and refers to Mark, also called John Mark. He was the son of Mary, the nephew of Barnabas, and a fellow traveler in ministry with Barnabas, Paul, and Peter. So Mark was a respected and very significant individual in the Early Church.

The name "Aristarchus" appears after Mark, and his name in Greek literally means *best ruler*. He was a Christian of Thessalonica and also a fellow prisoner with Paul. Like Demas, whose name is next in line, Aristarchus was from aristocracy, privilege, and wealth. Again, Demas was a companion and much-loved helper of the apostle Paul on his missionary journeys. As we've seen, some scholars believe it was Demas who received the dictation from Paul and penned what we've come to know as the book of Colossians.

"Luke" is the final person mentioned in the letter to Philemon, and as we've noted, he was a Christian physician as well as the writer of the gospel of Luke and the book of Acts. He, along with all the others mentioned before him, was a "fellowlaborer" with Paul. In Greek, this is the word *hoi sunergoi mou*, which is the plural form of *sunergos* with a definite article and the word *mou*. The word *sunergos* is a compound of the preposition *sun*, which means *together* and pictures *partnership*, and the word *ergon*, means *work* and pictures *production*. This brings us to the word *mou*, which means *of mine*, but when it's used with the definite article *hoi*, it means *THE fellow workers of mine*, stressing that these were the fellow team players who were associated with Paul.

This word "fellowlaborers" implies two people working closely together as partners sharing work and responsibility. There is even the notion of *equality* in the word, which means Epaphras, Mark, Aristarchus, Demas, and Luke were all Paul's fellow laborers or co-workers together with him. They were sharing the ministry and all the work it entailed. These men were all so respected that they shared a measure of equality among themselves. The point being made through all this is that Demas was a highly respected, high-level Christian leader among other Christian leaders of the same caliber.

In the End, Demas Abandoned Paul

The third mention of Demas comes in what we understand was Paul's final letter — the book of Second Timothy. As Paul was giving final instructions to his young spiritual son, he said, "Do thy diligence to come shortly unto me: For Demas hath forsaken me, having loved this present world, and is departed unto Thessalonica..." (2 Timothy 4:9,10). There are several key words we need to understand in these verses.

First is the word "diligence" — the Greek word *spoudadzo* — which means *to do something with haste because it is so important, serious, or urgent*. It can also mean *to give one's best efforts to a project or task and to do it enthusiastically*. The word "shortly" is the Greek word *tacheos*, which is from *tachus*, and it depicts *a runner who runs as fast as he can*. It carries the idea of *moving one's feet as fast as possible*, and it means *to do something urgently; to do something as swiftly as possible*.

Basically, Paul was telling Timothy to come to him as fast as he could, and the reason for the urgency was, Demas had "forsaken" him. In Greek, the word "forsaken" is *enkataleipo*, a compound of the prepositions *en* and *kata* and the word *leipo*. The preposition *en* means *in*; *kata* means *down*; and the word *leipo* means *to abandon, forsake*, or *leave behind*. When all three words are compounded, the new word *enkataleipo* — translated here as "forsaken" — means *to abandon, forsake*, or *leave in a bad situation*. This word not only means *to desert*, but also to do it in the worst way and at the worst possible moment. Hence, Demas didn't merely leave; he left Paul in the lurch at the worst possible moment.

What Motivated Demas' Departure?

Paul tells us in Second Timothy 4:10 that Demas, "having loved this present world," forsook him. The words "having loved" are a translation of the Greek word *agapesas*, which is from the word *agape*, and describes *the admiration one had for an object of beauty*. The onlooker was so taken by the object that it caused a deep admiration and appreciation to come out of his heart because he was so moved by what he had beheld. Normally, this word is used in the New Testament to describe the love of God and one's love for God. Here, however, it denotes Demas' love for *the world* — a love that he should have only felt for God.

This brings us to the phrase "present world," which is *ton nun aiona* in Greek. Here, the definite article *ton* is joined with the words *nun* and the word *aiona*. The word *nun* means *right now* or *the present moment*, and the word *aiona* depicts *an age with a concrete beginning and a concrete ending*, or *a measurable and limited age*. When these words are joined as a phrase, it denotes *the now age, this present age*, or *the here and now in this world*.

Finally, we have the word "departed," which in Greek is *poreuomai*. Here, it pictures *one who has departed or transitioned from a former position to another*. The implication is that Demas did not begin in a wrong place, but for some reason, he abandoned his former place or position to follow after a new place or position that was very different. So, he left his position as one of Paul's traveling companions and co-laborers and took on another position in Thessalonica.

Why Thessalonica?

The Scriptures do not say where Demas was from, but there are reasons to believe he was returning to his hometown of Thessalonica. It's likely that Thessalonica was a place where he had lived in comfort and pleasure, wealth, and prestige. Here we see the riches and comforts of this life were drawing Demas' heart away from God's calling.

John Chrysostom, an ancient Church leader, said, "…Having loved his own ease and security from danger, he chose rather to live luxuriously at home, than to suffer hardships." What's also interesting is that one scholar noted: A copyist in a manuscript preserved in the Medici Library in Florence added in the margin the information that Demas became a priest of a pagan temple at Thessalonica.

Can you imagine? Demas who had been highly trained by Paul and was serving side-by-side with him in the ministry of Jesus abandoned both Paul and the Lord in exchange for a life in the city of Thessalonica. The implication is Demas did not want to be a martyr, so he abandoned both Paul and the Lord.

What Can We Learn From Demas?

First, we should live with an eternal perspective on life and not be in love with this present world. Love for the ways, systems, and luxuries of this dying world pulls us away from our love for our living God and His Word. The second vital takeaway from Demas' example is that no Christian is immune from loving this present world and making a wrong decision.

In our next lesson, we will address the reason so many people today are falling into deception and what we can do to guard ourselves from falling into the same trap.

STUDY QUESTIONS

Study to shew thyself approved unto God, a workman that
needeth not to be ashamed, rightly dividing the word of truth.
— 2 Timothy 2:15

1. Prior to this lesson, had you ever heard of Demas? Does his story remind you of anyone else in Scripture? If so, who?

2. What is it about Demas' character that most surprised you? Have you ever found yourself in Paul's shoes, abandoned at the worst time and in the worst way by someone you fully expected to stay with you? What happened?

3. Take a few moments to reflect on the parable of the sower in Mark 4:1-20 (*see also* Matthew 13:1-23 and Luke 8:4-15). Which type of soil do you think best describes your heart?

PRACTICAL APPLICATION

> But be ye doers of the word, and not hearers only,
> deceiving your own selves.
> — James 1:22

1. When you consider Demas' "love for this present world," what kinds of things do you think sidetracked him? What things tend to dazzle and sidetrack you from following Jesus wholeheartedly?

2. On a similar note, what cares and concerns of the world often tie you up in worry and anxiety for yourself and your loved ones? Take a look at Matthew 6:25-34, really considering what Jesus is saying. In prayer, tell Him a few of the worries that weigh on your mind and invite Him to pull those "weeds" out of your thinking so you can breathe and grow freely.

LESSON 2

TOPIC

The Apostate Church at the End of the Age

SCRIPTURES

1. **2 Timothy 4:9,10** — Do thy diligence to come shortly unto me: For Demas hath forsaken me, having loved this present world, and is departed unto Thessalonica....

2. **1 Timothy 4:1** — Now the Spirit speaketh expressly, that in the latter times some shall depart from the faith, giving heed to seducing spirits, and doctrines of devils.

GREEK WORDS

1. "diligence" — σπουδάζω (*spoudadzo*): to do something with haste because it is so important, serious, or urgent; to give one's best efforts to a project or task and to do it enthusiastically

2. "shortly" — ταχέως (*tacheos*): from ταχύς (*tachus*); depicts a runner who runs as fast as he can; to move one's feet as fast as possible; to do something urgently; to do something as swiftly as possible

3. "Demas" — Δημᾶς (*Demas*): a companion and helper of the apostle Paul; here, spoken of with commendation as one in whom the apostle had confidence; some scholars believe that Demas was the one who actually penned the book of Colossians as it was dictated by Paul; he was likely from aristocracy, privilege, and wealth

4. "forsaken" — ἐγκαταλείπω (*enkataleipo*): a compound of the prepositions ἐν (*en*) and κατά (*kata*), and the word λείπω (*leipo*); the preposition ἐν (*en*) means in, κατά (*kata*) means down, and the word λείπω (*leipo*) means to abandon, forsake, or leave behind; as a compound, to abandon, forsake, or leave in a bad situation; not only to desert, but to do it in the worst way and at the worst possible moment; not merely to leave, but to leave in the lurch

5. "having loved" — ἀγαπήσας (*agapesas*): from the word ἀγάπη (*agape*); describes the admiration one had for an object of beauty; the onlooker was so taken by the object that it caused a deep admiration and appreciation to come out of his heart because he was so moved by what he had beheld; used in the New Testament to describe the love of God and one's love for God; here, however, Demas loved the world with a love that he should have only felt for God

6. "present world" — τὸν νῦν αἰῶνα (*ton nun aiona*): the definite article τὸν (*ton*) with νῦν (*nun*) and the word αἰῶνα (*aiona*); the word νῦν (*nun*) means right now or the present moment, and the word αἰῶνα (*aiona*) depicts an age with a concrete beginning and a concrete ending, or a measurable and limited age; as a phrase, the now age, this present age, or the here and now in this world

7. departed" — πορεύομαι (*poreuomai*): here, pictures one who has departed or transitioned from a former position to another; the implication is

Demas did not begin in a wrong place, but for some reason, he abandoned his former place or position to follow after a new place or position that was very different

8. "expressly" — ῥητῶς (*rhetos*): something spoken clearly or something that is unquestionable, certain, and sure; thus, what the Holy Spirit "expressly" says is definitely going to take place

9. "latter" — ὕστερος (*husteros*): later; pictures the ultimate end or the very last of something

10. "times" — καιρός (*kairos*): a season, time, or opportunity

11. "depart" — ἀφίστημι (*aphistemi*): a compound of ἀπό (*apo*) and ἵστημι (*histimi*); ἀπό (*apo*) means away, and ἵστημι (*histimi*) means to stand; compounded, they form the word ἀφίστημι (*aphistemi*), which means to stand apart from; to distance one's self from; to step away from; to withdraw from; or to shrink away from; it is from this very Greek word that we derive the word "apostate" or "apostasy"

12. "the faith" — πίστεως (*pisteos*): used here with a definite article, which means it refers to doctrine or the long-held, time-tested teachings of Scripture; thus, at the very end of the age, some will depart from the clear teaching of Scripture; little by little, they will distance themselves from God's truth and embrace something new that has captured their attention

13. "giving heed" — προσέχω (*prosecho*): a compound of πρός (*pros*), which means to lean toward, and ἔχω (*echo*), which means to hold or to embrace; when compounded, it pictures a person who has believed one thing for a very long time but is now leaning in a new direction to embrace something else; slowly but surely, they have released and withdrawn from what they once held precious and dear and have begun to hold on to new ideas and a new system of belief

14. "seducing [spirits]" — πλανάω (*planao*): to wander; pictures deception or a moral wandering; a person (or nation) that has veered from a solid path; as a result of veering morally, this person is adrift; also used to depict a lost animal that cannot find its path; to morally lose one's bearings; to wander off course

15. "devils" — δαιμόνιον (*daimonion*): evil spirits; demons; devils; the ancient world believed demons were the primary cause of disasters, suffering, and actions of insanity

SYNOPSIS

When Jesus' disciples pulled Him aside and asked what the sign would be of His coming and the end of the age, the first words out of Jesus' mouth were, "…Take heed that no man deceive you" (Matthew 24:4). The greatest sign that we have reached the last of the last days is widespread, worldwide *deception* — including deception in the Church. This raises two major questions and explains the purpose of this series: How can we guard ourselves from being caught in the sinister snare of deception, and how can we help rescue those who are caught in its grip?

The emphasis of this lesson:

The Holy Spirit prophesied through Paul that at the very end of the age, some believers would gradually step away from the time-tested truth of Scripture and begin to embrace the deceptive doctrine of demonic spirits.

A Brief Recap of Lesson 1

Demas was initially a devoted disciple.

As we saw in Lesson 1, Demas was first mentioned in Colossians 4:14, where Paul closed his letter by saying, "Luke, the beloved physician, and Demas, greet you." At that moment in time, Paul called Demas "beloved," meaning *one who is deeply cherished, admired*, and *appreciated*. This same level of sentiment is also seen in Paul's letter to Philemon, where he salutes and celebrates Demas as his "fellow laborer" and "fellow prisoner in Christ Jesus" along with other notable Christian leaders — John Mark, Aristarchus, and Luke the physician and writer.

Paul requested Timothy's urgent help.

When we come to the third and final mention of Demas, we discover that something shocking and tragic has taken place. Writing from his prison cell in the city of Rome, Paul urged Timothy, "Do thy diligence to come shortly unto me" (2 Timothy 4:9). We saw that the word "diligence" in Greek is *spoudadzo*, and it means *to do something with haste because it is so important, serious, or urgent*. It's the idea of giving one's best efforts to a project or task and to do it enthusiastically. The use of this word is the equivalent of Paul saying, "Timothy, make every effort to get here fast because the situation is seriously urgent."

We know this was the case because Paul added the word "shortly," which is the Greek word *tacheos*, from the word *tachus*, depicting *a runner who runs as fast as he can*. This term carries the idea of *moving one's feet as fast as possible* or *doing something urgently*. It means to do something as swiftly as possible. The fact that Paul used this word is like him saying, "I'm in a difficult place, so I need you to move your feet as fast as you can and get here quickly."

At some point, Demas deserted Paul.

The reason for the urgency is revealed in Second Timothy 4:10, where Paul states, "For Demas hath forsaken me, having loved this present world, and is departed unto Thessalonica...." The word "for" carries the idea of *shock* and *surprise*. It's like Paul was saying, "Amazing! Who would have ever imagined it? Can you believe it? I'm stunned by this turn of events..."

The fact that Demas abandoned Paul was dumbfounding. Remember, this was the renowned "Demas" who had been Paul's travel companion and helper — the one that scholars believe likely penned the book of Colossians as it was dictated by Paul. Demas was saluted and celebrated along with Luke, John Mark, and Aristarchus. How could this notable Christian leader have *forsaken* Paul and just "jumped ship" after serving the Lord for so long?

It was at the worst time, in the worst way.

In Greek, the word "forsaken" is a translation of the word *enkataleipo*, which is a compound of the prepositions *en* and *kata*, and the word *leipo*. The preposition *en* means *in*; kata means *down*; and the word *leipo* means *to abandon, forsake*, or *leave behind*. When compounded to form *enkataleipo*, it means *to abandon, forsake*, or *leave in a bad situation*. Not only does it mean to desert, but also to do it in the worst way and at the worst possible moment. Rather than merely leave, this is to leave someone in the lurch. By using this word, Paul is saying, "At the worst possible moment, in the worst possible way, Demas deserted me."

Demas was in love with the things of the world.

The reason for Demas' untimely departure is revealed in Second Timothy 4:10, where Paul said "...[Demas], having loved this present world, and is departed unto Thessalonica...." The phrase "having loved" is the Greek word *agapesas*, from the word *agape*; and it describes *the admiration one had for an object of beauty.* The onlooker was so taken by the object that it caused a deep admiration and appreciation to come out of his heart because he was so moved by what he had beheld. Normally, this word is used in the New Testament to describe *the love of God* and *one's love for God.* Here, however, it shows Demas loved the world with a love that he should have only felt for God.

The use of this word indicates that Demas had never gotten the world out of his heart. Even though he was serving the Lord and in ministry, there was something in him that was still obsessed with what the world was offering. He looked at the world and the things it offered with appreciation and a deep sense of value. He just couldn't shake his captivation of it. Again, believers should never use the word *agape* to describe anything except their love for God, the love for the Church, and the love for the brethren.

Nevertheless, Paul tells us that Demas had an inappropriate love and infatuation with the "present world." In Greek, "present world" is a translation of the phrase *ton nun aiona.* It features the definite article *ton* with *nun* and the word *aiona.* The word *nun* means *right now* or *the present moment,* and the word *aiona* depicts *an age with a concrete beginning and a concrete ending,* or *a measurable and limited age.* When these three words are joined as a phrase, it describes *the now age, this present age,* or *the here and now in this world.*

Demas returned to what was comfortable and familiar.

Although Demas had been trained by Paul and served at his side for quite some time as a notable Church leader, the Bible says that he "…departed unto Thessalonica…" (2 Timothy 4:10). The word "departed" is the Greek word *poreuomai,* and here it pictures *one who has departed or transitioned from a former position to another.* The implication is that Demas did not begin in a wrong place, but for some reason, he abandoned his former place or position to follow a new place or position that was very different. He abandoned his faith as well as his loyalty to Paul and his devotion to the Lord.

Why did Demas go to Thessalonica?

It seems that Demas was originally from Thessalonica, and his background was one of privilege, wealth, and aristocracy. By returning to Thessalonica, he returned to an environment that was comfortable. The truth is, sometimes serving the Lord really costs you a great deal. Many who enter ministry have high hopes of enjoying what they do as they devote their lives to serving the

Lord. But when they run into opposition again and again, they realize that sometimes serving the Lord is very uncomfortable, and they begin to think back on and yearn for how life used to be.

Apparently, that's what Demas did, and because he had never totally purged the love of the world from his heart, the thought of returning to Thessalonica was a viable option. Indeed, returning to Thessalonica was not only comfortable but also made it easy for him to blend into the surroundings and remain unnoticed. More than likely, Thessalonica was where Demas' family lived, and when he returned there, they would have rejoiced at his homecoming.

Moreover, returning to Thessalonica meant avoiding the ongoing opposition and pressure from sharing the Gospel with people in the world. The suffering would cease as he disappeared into the crowd away from his Christian friends and the Christian community. In fact, he could blend into the pagan environment of Thessalonica so well that his Christian friends wouldn't be able to find him.

After Paul's mention of Demas in his second letter to Timothy, there is nothing else said about him in the New Testament. He just disappears from the pages. Still, John Chrysostom, an early Christian leader, wrote about Demas and said, "…Having loved his own ease and security from danger, he chose rather to live luxuriously at home, than to suffer hardships."

One scholar noted: A copyist in a manuscript preserved in the Medici Library in Florence added in the margin the information that Demas became a priest of a pagan temple at Thessalonica. So rather than just go home, it appears Demas became a pagan priest, which was very praiseworthy in the pagan world. Those who became pagan priests enjoyed great status, which seems to be what Demas stepped into after abandoning Paul.

Demas' life is a sobering wake-up call to each of us that no Christian — regardless of how anointed or biblically wise we are — is immune from being distracted and deceived by the lure of this present age. Love for the world draws us away from our love for the Lord and His Word. Therefore, we should live with an eternal perspective on life and not be in love with this present world.

A Prophetic Picture of the Church in the Last Days

It is interesting that in Paul's first letter to Timothy, he wrote about what would take place at the end of the age. Under the inspiration of the Holy Spirit, Paul said in First Timothy 4:1, "Now the Spirit speaketh expressly, that in the latter times some shall depart from the faith, giving heed to seducing spirits, and doctrines of devils." The original Greek meaning of this text is truly remarkable.

For example, the word "expressly" in Greek is *rhetos*, which is from the word *rhema*, and it describes *something spoken clearly or something that is unquestionable, certain, and sure*. Thus, what the Holy Spirit says "expressly" is definitely going to take place. It's not optional or simply a possibility. What He's prophesying here is *most certainly* going to happen.

When will this take place? In the "latter times." The word "latter" is the Greek word *husteros*, which means *later* and pictures *the ultimate end or the very last of something*. The word "times" here is the Greek word *kairos*, which describes *a season, time, or opportunity*. The indication from these two words is that *at the very end of the age*, there will be *opportunities* for "…some [to] depart from the faith…" (1 Timothy 4:1).

The word "depart" in Greek is *aphistemi*, a compound of *apo* and *histimi*. The word *apo* means *away*, and *histimi* means *to stand*. When compounded, they form the word *aphistemi*, which means *to stand apart from* or *to distance one's self from*. It can also be translated *to step away from*; *to withdraw from*; or *to shrink away from*. It is from this very Greek word that we derive the word "apostate" or "apostasy."

"Departing" and "rejecting" are different. Notice this verse doesn't say people will *reject* the faith. It says they will *depart* — or *stray* — from the faith. Rejecting is *abrupt* and *deliberate*, while departing is *slow* and could even be *unintentional*. There is a huge difference between the two. The use of this word *aphistemi* — translated here as "depart" — implies that at the very end of the age, we are going to encounter a season when believers inside the Church will begin *to gradually step away and shrink back from what they once believed*.

Specifically, Paul prophesied that believers would depart from "the faith," which is the Greek word *pisteos* used here with a definite article. This is important because it refers to *doctrine* or *the long-held, time-tested teachings of Scripture.* Thus, at the very end of the age, some will depart from *the clear teaching of Scripture.* Little by little, they will distance themselves from God's truth and embrace something new that has captured their attention.

People will listen to seducing spirits. As these believers are gradually stepping away from truth, they will be "giving heed to seducing spirits" (*see* 1 Timothy 4:1). The words "giving heed" are a translation of the Greek word *prosecho.* This is a compound of the word *pros,* which means *to lean toward,* and the word *echo,* which means *to hold or to embrace.* When compounded to form *prosecho,* it pictures *a person who has believed one thing for a very long time but is now leaning in a new direction to embrace something else.* Slowly but surely, they have released and withdrawn from what they once held precious and dear and have begun to hold on to new ideas and a new system of belief.

Paul declared that at the end of the age, there will be a temptation for some to depart from the clear, sound teaching of Scripture. They're going to open their minds to new ideas and new concepts and slowly turn from what they once believed — putting distance between themselves and the truth of God's Word they once proclaimed — in order to embrace what Paul calls *seducing spirits* and *doctrines of demons.*

In Greek, the word "seducing" is the word *planao,* which means *to wander.* It pictures *deception* or *a moral wandering of a person (or nation) that has veered from a solid path.* As a result of veering morally, this person is adrift. Interestingly, this word *planao* was also used to depict a lost animal that cannot find its path back home. Essentially, it means *to morally lose one's bearings* or *to wander off course.*

This brings us to the word "devils" — the Greek word *daimonion* — which refers to *evil spirits, demons, or devils.* The ancient world believed demons were the primary cause of disasters, suffering, and actions of insanity. Doctrines of devils will abound in the last-days society and cause many to become morally insane.

This is happening right now. More than likely, you are aware of major Christian leaders who at this very moment are distancing themselves from the time-tested truth of Scripture. One well-known leader is even saying that the Church should unhitch from the Bible and that the Scripture many have built their faith upon is a house of cards that's going to crumble. This same recognized minister is also beginning to embrace immoral things as normal that are not in agreement with Scripture.

There is also a major Christian denomination that will soon begin blessing same-sex unions. The truth is, we saw this coming a long time ago. The major Christian leader — who is as notable today as Demas was in the Early Church — didn't just reject the faith overnight; he departed very slowly. The Holy Spirit said these kinds of things would happen, and we are seeing it now with our own eyes.

Friend, beware of trying to be so "open-minded" or "progressive thinking" that you begin to step away from the clear, sound teaching of God's Word. It can happen to anyone — including you. Seducing spirits and doctrines of demons are whispering messages and proclaiming perversity that is causing people to morally wander from the narrow way. The only remedy for this reckless insanity is to stay rooted daily in the Word.

In our third lesson, we will look at what we need to do to resist the pressure to give in to and accommodate the world's ungodly demands.

STUDY QUESTIONS

Study to shew thyself approved unto God, a workman that needeth not to be ashamed, rightly dividing the word of truth.
— 2 Timothy 2:15

1. When you read the phrases "seducing spirits" and "doctrines of devils," what comes to mind? Did it ever dawn on you that some of the messages we all hear on an everyday basis might be coming from the enemy? How does this sobering reality cause you to adjust your thinking?

2. Sometimes Satan's lies don't look or sound like lies. What did Paul and John say about appearances when it comes to the Gospel? How should we respond when someone preaches a message that's not consistent with Scripture? (Consider Galatians 1:8,9 and 1 John 4:1-6 as you answer.)

PRACTICAL APPLICATION

But be ye doers of the word, and not hearers only, deceiving your own selves.
—James 1:22

1. Have you ever found yourself believing one of the enemy's lies? What was it? How did you come to the realization that something you were believing wasn't right?

2. Who is someone you know (or know of) that has gradually fallen away from the truth of Scripture? Which issue or truth in Scripture did he or she let go of first? What do that person's choices cause you to step back and reevaluate in your own life?

3. Take a moment to invite the Holy Spirit to show you what lies you might be believing right now, and to give you the grace to learn and hold on to the unchanging truth of Scripture. (Consider Psalm 139:23,24; James 4:6; and Psalm 84:11.)

LESSON 3

TOPIC

Resisting the Pressure To Accommodate the World

SCRIPTURES

1. **2 Timothy 4:9,10** — Do thy diligence to come shortly unto me: For Demas hath forsaken me, having loved this present world, and is departed unto Thessalonica....

2. **Revelation 2:13-16** — I know thy works, and where thou dwellest, even where Satan's seat is: and thou holdest fast my name, and hast not denied my faith, even in those days wherein Antipas was my faithful martyr, who was slain among you, where Satan dwelleth. But I have a few things against thee, because thou hast there them that hold the doctrine of Balaam, who taught Balac to cast a stumblingblock before the children of Israel, to eat things sacrificed to idols, and to commit fornication. So hast thou also them that hold the doctrine of the Nicolaitanes, which thing I hate. Repent; or else I will come unto thee quickly, and will fight against them with the sword of my mouth.

3. **1 Timothy 4:1** — Now the Spirit speaketh expressly, that in the latter times some shall depart from the faith, giving heed to seducing spirits, and doctrines of devils.

GREEK WORDS

1. "diligence"— **σπουδάζω** (*spoudadzo*): to do something with haste because it is so important, serious, or urgent; to give one's best efforts to a project or task and to do it enthusiastically

2. "shortly"— **ταχέως** (*tacheos*): from **ταχύς** (*tachus*); depicts a runner who runs as fast as he can; to move one's feet as fast as possible; to do something urgently; to do something as swiftly as possible

3. "Demas"— **Δημᾶς** (*Demas*): a companion and helper of the apostle Paul; here, spoken of with commendation as one in whom the apostle had confidence; some scholars believe that Demas was the one who actually penned the book of Colossians as it was dictated by Paul; he was likely from aristocracy, privilege, and wealth

4. "forsaken"— **ἐγκαταλείπω** (*enkataleipo*): a compound of the prepositions **ἐν** (*en*) and **κατά** (*kata*), and the word **λείπω** (*leipo*); the preposition **ἐν** (*en*) means in, **κατά** (*kata*) means down, and the word **λείπω** (*leipo*) means to abandon, forsake, or leave behind; as a compound, to abandon, forsake, or leave in a bad situation; not only to desert, but to do it in the worst way and at the worst possible moment; not merely to leave, but to leave in the lurch

5. "present world"— **τὸν νῦν αἰῶνα** (*ton nun aiona*): the definite article **τὸν** (*ton*) with **νῦν** (*nun*) and the word **αἰῶνα** (*aiona*); the word **νῦν** (*nun*) means right now or the present moment, and the word **αἰῶνα** (*aiona*) depicts an age with a concrete beginning and a concrete ending, or a measurable and limited age; as a phrase, the now age, this present age, or the here and now in this world

6. "departed"— **πορεύομαι** (*poreuomai*): here, pictures one who has departed or transitioned from a former position to another; the implication is Demas did not begin in a wrong place, but for some reason, he abandoned his former place or position to follow after a new place or position that was very different

7. Antipas — **Ἀντιπᾶς** (*Antipas*): a compound of **ἀντί** (*anti*), which means against, and **πᾶς** (*pas*), which means all; when compounded, the name Antipas actually means one who is against all; this word can figuratively describe a person who is against everything

8. "Nicolaitans"— **Νικόλαος** (*Nikolaos*): a compound of **νῖκος** (*nikos*), which means to conquer, and the word (*laos*), which depicts people or

the laity; as a compound, to conquer and subdue people; a name that depicts one who conquers and subdues people

9. "hate" — μισέω (*miseo*): to hate, abhor, or find utterly repulsive; depicts a deep-seated animosity; intense hatred; repugnance; something objectionable; pictures something that causes one to feel disgust or repulsion; a deep-seated aversion; it is not just dislike, but actual hatred

SYNOPSIS

There is a fascinating scripture in the Bible that says, "History merely repeats itself. It has all been done before. Nothing under the sun is truly new" (Ecclesiastes 1:9 *NLT*). Oh, how true! What happened in the Early Church is happening again in the Last-Days Church. Just as believers were gradually distancing themselves from the truth then, they are doing the same thing now. The life of Demas is a perfect example.

But just because apostasy is taking place today, it doesn't mean you have to fall victim to it. God has made a way — through the power of His Holy Spirit and His unchanging Word — to help you maintain a sound mind and not give in to the insanity of seducing spirits and doctrines of demons. In fact, you can even help others escape the pitfalls of perversity, which is what we will see in this lesson.

The emphasis of this lesson:

What was going on in the church of Pergamum in the First Century is the same thing taking place in many churches today. The doctrine of Balaam and the doctrine of the Nicolaitans are being repeated all over again. But with God's help, we can refuse to compromise and accommodate people's sinful lifestyles, and we can hold firm to the standards of Scripture.

A BRIEF RECAP OF LESSONS 1 AND 2

In our first two lessons, we examined the life of Demas, a notable, First Century Christian leader who is mentioned in the New Testament in three places. In Colossians 4:14, Paul includes Demas and Luke in his closing salutation, referring to both as "beloved." As a traveling companion and assistant to Paul, Demas was *deeply cherished, admired, and appreciated.* In a similar way, Demas is also celebrated in Philemon 23 and 24 right alongside other notable leaders. In this verse, Paul mentions:

- **Epaphras,** the leader of the Colossian church
- **Mark,** who wrote the book of Mark and was a traveling companion of Barnabas and Paul, and the son of Mary and the nephew of Barnabas
- **Aristarchus,** a great Christian leader
- **Luke,** the Christian physician, and writer of the book of Luke and the book of Acts

Right in the middle of all these great leaders, we find Demas mentioned as Paul's "fellow prisoner" and "fellow laborer." Clearly, at that time, Demas too, was a very notable, effective leader.

However, something happened along the way that caused Demas to go AWOL. We know this to be a fact because Paul wrote to Timothy and said, "Do thy *diligence* to come shortly unto me" (2 Timothy 4:9). The word "diligence" in Greek is *spoudadzo*, and it means *to do something with haste because it is so important, serious, or urgent.* The word "shortly" is the Greek word *tacheos*, from the word *tachus*, and it depicts *a runner who runs as fast as he can.* It carries the idea of *moving one's feet as fast as possible, doing something urgently*, or *doing something as swiftly as possible.* At the time of this writing, Paul was in prison in Rome, and he urgently needed help.

The reason? Paul said, "For Demas hath forsaken me, having loved this present world, and is departed unto Thessalonica..." (2 Timothy 4:10). The word "for" carries the idea of *shock* and *surprise.* Paul was absolutely stunned that Demas had forsaken him. This was the same Demas who had been Paul's traveling companion and had likely written the book of Colossians as Paul dictated it.

Astonished and bewildered, Paul informed Timothy that Demas had "forsaken" him. We saw that "forsaken" is a translation of the word *enkataleipo*, which means *to abandon, forsake*, or *leave in a bad situation.* Not only does it mean to desert, but also to do it in the worst way and at the worst time possible. Rather than merely leave, Demas left Paul *in the lurch.*

What caused Demas to desert Paul? The Bible says, "...[Demas] having loved this present world, and is departed unto Thessalonica..." (2 Timothy 4:10). This passage informs us that Demas had an unhealthy love and infatuation with the "present world." In Greek, "present world" describes *the now age, this present age,* or *the here and now in this world.* And the word "departed" is the Greek word *poreuomai*, which pictures *one who has departed or transitioned from a former* *position to another.* The use of this word indicates that Demas didn't begin in a wrong place, but for some reason, he abandoned his former place or position to follow a new place or position that was very different. He left not only Paul, but also his faith and loyalty to Jesus.

Jesus Is Well Aware of What's Going on in His Church

It is important to realize that God is fully aware of each person's level of devotion to Him. We see this fact clearly in the way Jesus speaks to the seven churches in the book of Revelation. For example, in Revelation 2:13, Jesus is addressing the church in Pergamum, and He says:

> **I know thy works, and where thou dwellest, even where Satan's seat is: and thou holdest fast my name, and hast not denied my faith, even in those days wherein Antipas was my faithful martyr, who was slain among you, where Satan dwelleth.**

There are some important words to understand in this passage — starting with the word "know." It is a form of the Greek word *oida*, which means *to know, to understand*, or *to comprehend*, and it is *a firsthand knowledge based on personal observation.* The word "works" is also significant. It is the Greek word *ergon*, which describes *all of one's work, activities, and behavior.* The use of these words is the equivalent of Jesus saying, "There's not a thing about you that I don't know. I've personally been with you and observed everything you've done — and are doing — with My own eyes."

Jesus went on to tell the pastor and people of the church in Pergamum, "I know thy works, and where thou dwellest…" (Revelation 2:13). The same is true of us — Jesus is personally acquainted with all our works and activities and is aware of where we live. For the church in Pergamum, He said that He knew that they were living, "…even where Satan's seat is…" (Revelation 2:13).

History reveals that the city of Pergamum was a very wicked, dark city, so it's not surprising that Jesus called it the "seat of Satan." Interestingly, the Greek word for "seat" that's used here is the word *thronos.* This is where we get the word "throne," which tells us Satan's throne was in Pergamum, and he was ruling like a king from that particular city. Furthermore, the word *thronos* — here translated "seat" — was the very word used in the Greek language to describe *the seat reserved for the head of the house at the table.* No one else would dare to sit in that seat because it belonged exclusively to the head of the house. By using this word, Jesus was saying, "I know the devil thinks he's the head of the house in the city of Pergamum and he's exercising his authority from there…."

The People Viewed All Christians as 'Antipas'

Looking again at Revelation 2:13, Jesus went on to tell the church of Pergamum:

> **…And thou holdest fast my name, and hast not denied my faith, even in those days wherein Antipas was my faithful martyr, who was slain among you, where Satan dwelleth.**

If we carefully read this portion of the text, we can deduce that Jesus was talking about a very unique time in the history of that church and city when certain memorable events took place. Then He specifically mentions that Antipas was martyred during that time. The name "Antipas" — from the Greek word *Antipas* — is a compound of the word *anti*, which means *against*, and *pas*, which means *all*. When these words are compounded, the name *Antipas* actually means *one who is against all*. This word can figuratively describe a person who is against everything.

Indeed, the opinion of the people of Pergamum about this man Antipas was that he was against everything. What's worse is that they thought this way about all Christians. Because of the believers' separation from the world, the opinion of the dark, unbelieving world of Pergamum was that all Christians were antisocial, contrary, noncompliant, intolerant, narrow-minded, nonconformist, inflexible, obstinate, and uncompromising.

Does that sound familiar? That is exactly how many people in the world view us as Christians. The world calls us antisocial because we don't just go with the flow. They often view us as contrary, noncompliant intolerant, narrow-minded, nonconformist, inflexible, obstinate, and uncompromising. It's history repeating itself once again.

The 'Doctrine of Balaam' Was at Work in the Church of Pergamum

Now when we come to Revelation 2:14, we see that there was a certain group of people in the church of Pergamum that Jesus was very upset with, which is why He told them:

But I have a few things against thee, because thou hast there them that hold the doctrine of Balaam, who taught Balac to cast a stumblingblock before the children of Israel, to eat things sacrificed to idols, and to commit fornication.

"What is the doctrine of Balaam?" you might ask. Balaam was a false prophet who tried to curse the people of Israel in an effort to receive financial gain from Balak, king of Moab. Although he tried and tried and tried, he was unable to curse what God had blessed. Then after much thought, Balaam's twisted mind concocted a plan to bring evil upon the Israelites.

"Seeing as I can't curse them directly," he basically told King Balak, "We can get them to bring a curse on themselves by luring them into moral compromise. Send the pagan women out naked before the Israelite men who haven't seen their wives for a long time, and have the women dance in front of the men, luring them into sexual sin and into making sacrifices to the pagan gods."

Balaam's scheme worked. The men of Israel dropped their guard, pursued the pagan women, and ended up offering sacrifices to false gods (*see* Numbers 25:1-3; 31:16). Thus, the doctrine of Balaam mentioned in Revelation 2:14 is *moral and spiritual compromise.*

The 'Doctrine of the Nicolaitans' Was Also Embraced at the Church of Pergamum

Jesus continued His message to the church at Pergamum saying, "So hast thou also them that hold the doctrine of the Nicolaitanes, which thing I hate" (Revelation 2:15). The word "Nicolaitanes" (or Nicolaitans) in Greek is *Nikolaos*. It is a compound of the word *nikos*, which means *to conquer,* and the word *laos*, which depicts *people* or *the laity*. When these words are compounded to form *Nikolaos*, it means *to conquer and subdue people.* That is what this name depicts — *one who conquers and subdues people.*

Whatever these false teachers in Pergamum were teaching was influencing believers to compromise with the world. Indeed, the Nicolaitan doctrine was conquering and defeating God's people at Pergamum. Their message basically said:

> We need to relax our rules! Rather than live so separate from the rest of the world, we need to befriend the world — to go

where they go, do what they do, learn to speak their language, to be more like them — so they will be more accepting of us and our message. It's time for us to quit drawing lines and to start drawing bigger circles so we become more loving and accepting and inclusive of others!

Friend, if anyone tells you it's time to stop drawing biblical lines, they're preaching a false Gospel. Jesus drew many lines when He was interacting with people. He showed compassion, yet clearly defined what was right and what was wrong, and the line was never blurred. Rather than draw bigger circles and widen the way to include more people and make them feel comfortable, Jesus said, "…Narrow is the gate and difficult is the way which leads to life, and there are few who find it" (Matthew 7:14 *NKJV*). He calls us to repentance, to live a holy, set apart life, and to build and pursue His Kingdom above our own.

Any time we broaden the lines to accept people's ungodly behaviors and lifestyles that are against Scripture, just to make them feel more comfortable, we're off track and heading down the path to hypocrisy. This is what the Nicolaitans were doing: trying to accommodate the world rather than call them to a higher way of living and to change. Can you see why Jesus was so upset with the people in the church of Pergamum who were tolerating the teaching of the Nicolaitans?

Again, when speaking of the doctrine of the Nicolaitans, Jesus said it is "…[the] thing I hate" (Revelation 2:15). Although He didn't say He hated the people, He did say He hated what they were teaching and endorsing. The word "hate" in this passage is the Greek word *miseo*, which means *to hate, to abhor,* or *to find utterly repulsive.* It depicts *a deep-seated animosity; intense hatred; repugnance;* or *something objectionable.* It pictures something that causes one to feel disgust or repulsion. It is a deep-seated aversion — it is not just dislike, but actual hatred.

Signs of Present-Day Nicolaitanism

Without question, the doctrine of the Nicolaitans is alive and well today. When you read through their basic message, you can hear how similar it is to the mindsets and messages being put forth by several denominations as well as known and unknown ministers.

Present-day Nicolaitanism…

- Puts no emphasis on living holy and separated from the world. The lines are blurred.

- Places no value on the doctrinal integrity and teaching of the Bible. In fact, it says we need to "unhitch" from Scripture and quit quoting it all the time.

- Puts no emphasis on absolute truth or absolute biblical authority. In fact, it even works to diminish biblical authority.

- Holds no exclusionary belief that Christ alone is the way to Heaven.

An example of this would be a well-known pastor who recently said, "Jesus said He is the only way, but just because He said that doesn't necessarily mean it's true." Do you see and understand the gravity of that statement? This person is diminishing the supreme lordship of Jesus Christ, who said, "…I am **the way, the truth**, and **the life**: no man cometh unto the Father, but by me" (John 14:6). Again, Jesus hates this kind of teaching — the doctrine of the Nicolaitans.

The Insanity in the World We're Seeing Is the Result of 'Seducing Spirits and Doctrines of Demons'

How did Jesus deal with those who were tolerating the doctrine of the Nicolaitans? He told them, "Repent; or else I will come unto thee quickly, and will fight against them with the sword of my mouth" (Revelation 2:16).

Notice Jesus said, "…I will come unto thee quickly.…" The words "unto thee" are translated from the Greek word *soi*, which means *directly to you*. The word "quickly" is the Greek word *tachus*, which causes Jesus' statement to sound more like, "I'm going to *move My feet as fast as I can* to get *directly to you*." Jesus said once He arrives, He will "fight against them with the sword of His mouth." The word "fight" in Greek is *polemos*, and it describes *an all-out war*. The word "sword" is the Greek word *rhomphaia*, which was the most vicious sword of all because it was used to *slaughter*. Essentially, Jesus said, "I'm going to slaughter these activities because I hate it and am against it."

Remember, the Holy Spirit prophesied through Paul about the conditions at the end of the age, saying, "Now the Spirit speaketh expressly, that in the latter times some shall depart from the faith, giving heed to seducing spirits, and doctrines of devils" (1 Timothy 4:1).

This departure from the faith is the doctrine of the Nicolaitans. When the Bible talks about "doctrines of devils," the word "doctrines" in Greek is *didaskalia*, which describes *well-packaged information*. The use of this word tells us the devil is going to come with the best PR campaign he's ever had, but it will be propagated by "devils." In Greek, the word "devils" is *daimoniōn*, which describes *spirits that lead to delusion and insanity*.

To a great degree, that is what we are seeing take place in churches all over the world right now. The celebration and sanctioning of same-sex marriage, gender fluidity, and the mutilation of children's reproductive organs is sheer demonic lunacy. The enemy is working overtime trying to lure people away from the narrow path of God's Word onto a broader path that's more accommodating and inclusive of others. These things are the result of seducing spirits and doctrines of demons, and they are *destructive*.

In our next lesson, we will examine three forces that try to lure you to abandon your faith.

STUDY QUESTIONS

> Study to shew thyself approved unto God, a workman that
> needeth not to be ashamed, rightly dividing the word of truth.
> — 2 Timothy 2:15

1. Have you ever heard about the "doctrine of Balaam" before? After reading that section, does it sound like anything happening today? Which Israelite leader fell into this trap himself on a huge scale (*see* 1 Kings 11:1-13)?
2. How do you think the doctrines of Balaam and of the Nicolaitans is working together currently to derail believers today?

PRACTICAL APPLICATION

> But be ye doers of the word, and not hearers only,
> deceiving your own selves.
> — James 1:22

1. When you consider the fact that Jesus knew everything that was going on in the church of Pergamum firsthand — just as He knows everything that is going on in each of our lives — does it make you

want to live differently? What do you really want Jesus to personally observe in *your* life as He is walking with you?

2. Think about Ecclesiastes 1:9 for a minute — how there's ultimately nothing new under the sun. It means believers across generations understand what it's like to be tempted by the enemy and to stand strong against his sinister schemes. Who is one older believer you can look to for advice on some of the challenges you're facing now? Take some time to reach out to that person and ask what he or she has learned over the years of fighting the good fight of faith. Invite the Holy Spirit to lead your conversation. He wants to help you and empower you with His grace to stay strong and experience victory in every area of your life.

LESSON 4

TOPIC
Three Forces That Try To Lure You To Abandon Your Faith

SCRIPTURES

1. **2 Timothy 4:9,10** — Do thy diligence to come shortly unto me: For Demas hath forsaken me, having loved this present world, and is departed unto Thessalonica....

2. **1 John 2:15,16** — Love not the world, neither the things that are in the world. If any man love the world, the love of the Father is not in him. For all that is in the world, the lust of the flesh, and the lust of the eyes, and the pride of life, is not of the Father, but is of the world.

3. **1 John 5:19** — ...The whole world lieth in wickedness.

4. **Psalm 101:3** — I will set no wicked thing before mine eyes: I hate the work of them that turn aside; it shall not cleave to me.

5. **Proverbs 28:16** (*NKJV*) — ...He who hates covetousness will prolong his days.

6. **Luke 12:15** (*NKJV*) — ...Take heed and beware of covetousness, for one's life does not consist in the abundance of the things he possesses.

7. **Psalm 119:37** (*NIV*) — Turn my eyes away from worthless things....

8. **1 John 2:17** — And the world passeth away, and the lust thereof: but he that doeth the will of God abideth for ever.

9. **1 Corinthians 10:12** (*NKJV*) — Therefore let him who thinks he stands take heed lest he fall.

GREEK WORDS

1. "diligence" — σπουδάζω (*spoudadzo*): to do something with haste because it is so important, serious, or urgent; to give one's best efforts to a project or task and to do it enthusiastically

2. "shortly" — ταχέως (*tacheos*): from ταχύς (*tachus*); depicts a runner who runs as fast as he can; to move one's feet as fast as possible; to do something urgently; to do something as swiftly as possible

3. "Demas" — Δημᾶς (*Demas*): a companion and helper of the apostle Paul; here, spoken of with commendation as one in whom the apostle had confidence; some scholars believe that Demas was the one who actually penned the book of Colossians as it was dictated by Paul; he was likely from aristocracy, privilege, and wealth

4. "forsaken" — ἐγκαταλείπω (*enkataleipo*): a compound of the prepositions ἐν (*en*) and κατά (*kata*), and the word λείπω (*leipo*); the preposition ἐν (*en*) means in, κατά (*kata*) means down, and the word λείπω (*leipo*) means to abandon, forsake, or leave behind; as a compound, to abandon, forsake, or leave in a bad situation; not only to desert, but to do it in the worst way and at the worst possible moment; not merely to leave, but to leave in the lurch

5. "departed" — πορεύομαι (*poreuomai*): here, pictures one who has departed or transitioned from a former position to another; the implication is Demas did not begin in a wrong place, but for some reason, he abandoned his former place or position to follow after a new place or position that was very different

6. "love" — ἀγαπάω (*agapao*): to deeply cherish, profoundly love, and treasure; depicts one that is so captivated by what he sees that he is nearly fixed and obsessed with it; it is used in a positive sense to denote the love of God and love we should have for one another

7. "world" — κόσμος (*kosmos*): the world; denotes systems and institutions in society, such as fashion, education, or entertainment; world systems; often used to denote a particular political system; systems in any part of society; the realm where Satan exercises his influence

8. "the things" — τὰ (*ta*): things; many things

9. "lust" — ἐπιθυμία (*epithumia*): from ἐπί (*epi*) and θυμός (*thumos*); the word ἐπί (*epi*) means over and gives intensity to the word; the word θυμός (*thumos*) is passionate desire; when these words are compounded to form ἐπιθυμία (*epithumia*), it describes desire, cravings, or a longing; one bent over and craving a thing

10. "flesh" — σαρκός (*sarkos*): flesh; carnal nature; base, fleshly instincts

11. "lust" — ἐπιθυμία (*epithumia*): from ἐπί (*epi*) and θυμός (*thumos*); the word ἐπί (*epi*) means over and gives intensity to the word; the word θυμός (*thumos*) is passionate desire; when these words are compounded to form ἐπιθυμία (*epithumia*), it describes desire, cravings, or a longing; one bent over and craving a thing

12. "eyes" — (*ophthalmos*): the eye; figuratively, the mind's eye

13. "pride" — ἀλαζών (*aladzon*): one full of himself; one who goes on about how great he is, as he tries to be or to look outwardly impressive; one who is obsessed with self-importance

SYNOPSIS

In today's world, sinful practices are celebrated. The enemy works tirelessly through the world's systems, painting highly deceptive portraits of pleasure, but he never reveals the price tag of our choices. Steal, kill, and destroy is his M.O., which is why the writer of Hebrews wrote to us and said, "…Warn (admonish, urge, and encourage) one another every day, as long as it is called Today, that none of you may be hardened [into settled rebellion] by the deceitfulness of sin [by the fraudulence, the stratagem, the trickery which the delusive glamor of his sin may play on him]" (Hebrews 3:13 *AMPC*). Indeed, sin is deceitful, but thankfully through the power of the Holy Spirit and the truth of God's Word, we can recognize Satan's lures and escape the delusive glamour of sin!

The emphasis of this lesson:

The enemy uses three primary types of temptation to try to sidetrack and derail us from our destiny. These are the lust of the flesh, the lust of the eyes, and the pride of life. God warns us not to be captivated by, fixated on, or obsessed with anything the world has to offer.

A Review of Our Anchor Verse

In our first three lessons, we've seen that Demas was a highly respected and dearly loved co-laborer with Paul. But something happened along the way that caused him to change direction. Paul writes about it in his second letter to Timothy, saying, "Do thy diligence to come shortly unto me: For Demas hath forsaken me, having loved this present world, and is departed unto Thessalonica…" (2 Timothy 4:9,10).

What did Paul ask of Timothy? Notice the word "diligence" in verse 9. It is the Greek word *spoudadzo*, and it means *to do something with haste because it is so important, serious, or urgent.* Paul's use of this word is the equivalent of him asking, "Please do this quickly because the situation is very serious." Paul urgently asked Timothy to come to him "shortly," which is the Greek word *tacheos*, from *tachus*, and it depicts *a runner who runs as fast as he can.* It is the idea of moving one's feet as fast as possible — so fast that his feet don't touch the ground at the same time. When we combine the meaning of these words, we see Paul was saying, "Move your feet as fast as you possibly can and get here."

Why was Paul so strong with his request? He says, "For Demas hath forsaken me, having loved this present world, and is departed unto Thessalonica…" (2 Timothy 4:10). The opening word "for" in Greek expresses shock and surprise. It's like Paul was saying, "Can you believe it? Who would have thought this would happen? Demas — my once beloved co-worker — has forsaken me."

Again, "Demas" was a companion and helper of the apostle Paul and was noted among other Christian leaders. Some scholars believe that Demas was the one who actually penned the book of Colossians as it was dictated by Paul. It's likely that he was from aristocracy, privilege, and wealth. But here, Paul said that this once trustworthy, reliable assistant had *forsaken* him.

This word "forsaken" is the Greek word *enkataleipo*, and it means *to abandon, forsake, or leave in a bad situation.* It is not only to desert, but to do it in the worst way and at the worst possible moment. Rather than to merely leave, this word means *to leave in the lurch.* In bewilderment, Paul told Timothy, "Could you ever have imagined that Demas — our beloved companion and co-worker — would abandon me? And he's done it in the worst way and at the worst time. Filled with love for this present world, he has departed unto Thessalonica…."

Why would Demas go to Thessalonica? More than likely, that is where he was from, and returning there meant returning to aristocracy, privilege, and wealth, which was a more comfortable lifestyle. Certainly, our walk of faith is sometimes uncomfortable, which may be what Demas was dealing with while traveling with Paul. It may be that he came to the realization that his faith was going to seriously cost him something, so he returned to where it was more comfortable and where he could easily blend into the atmosphere. In Thessalonica, he could disappear in the middle of a large pagan city and avoid the brunt of persecution. Other believers would not know where he was, so they couldn't seek him out. Overall, Demas could experience an easier life in Thessalonica.

Don't Love the World or the Things of the World

It is very important for us to see that Demas' love of the world is what lured him out of God's purpose and plan for his life. The apostle John warned us, "Love not the world, neither the things that are in the world. If any man love the world, the love of the Father is not in him" (1 John 2:15). To understand what John is saying, we need to define some of the key words here.

First, is the word "love," which is the Greek word *agapao*, and it means *to deeply cherish, profoundly love, and treasure*. It depicts one that is so captivated by what he sees that he is nearly fixed and obsessed with it. Hence, we could translate John's warning, "Treasure not and cherish not the world, neither the things that are in the world...."

Often, this word *agapao* (love) is used in a positive sense to denote the love of God and the love we should have for one another. But here it is used in a negative sense to warn us not to be captivated by, fixated on, or obsessed with the world and its things. This kind of profound, deep love for the world and its ways is misdirected and quite deadly.

The word "world" is the Greek word *kosmos*, and it describes *the world*, but especially denotes *organized systems and institutions in society*, such as *fashion, education*, or *entertainment*. Essentially, it is *world systems*, and often this word was used to denote *a particular political system* or *systems in any part of society*. In the Scriptures, the world (*kosmos*) is the realm where Satan operates and exercises his influence.

Second Corinthians 4:4 identifies Satan as "the god of this world," and the word "world" here is *kosmos*, which means he's the god of the *systems* of the world. Thus, he is not the god of the planet or the god of nature. He is the ruler of the systems and institutions in society, operating through things like politics, fashion, education, and entertainment. The world systems are like puppets in his hands.

That is why the Bible says, "Love not the world, neither the things that are in the world…" (1 John 2:15). In Greek, the phrase "the things" is the word *ta*, and it describes *things* or *many things* that are in the world. The word for "world" is again the Greek word *kosmos*, referring to *systems and institutions in society*. Hence, John is urging us not to treasure or be profoundly in love with the institutions and systems of this world.

The World Offers Three Categories of Temptation

John goes on to say, "For all that is in the world, the lust of the flesh, and the lust of the eyes, and the pride of life, is not of the Father, but is of the world" (1 John 2:16). The word "all" here is the Greek word *pan*, which is *all-inclusive* and depicts *everything* that is in the "world." Again, for the third time in two verses, we see the word *kosmos*, so when John talks about "all that is in the world," he means *everything that is rooted in world systems*.

Keep in mind "…that we are of God, and the whole world lieth in wickedness" (1 John 5:19). So since Satan is the god of this world and the whole world is steeped in wickedness, are you starting to see why the Holy Spirit prompted John to urge us not to love the world? To become captivated and obsessed with the world's ways of entertainment, politics, education, judicial rulings, and fashion is deadly — not to mention the fact that it is all passing away (*see* 1 John 2:17).

Interestingly, when you look at First John 2:16, it tells us **all that is in the world falls into three basic categories**: *the lust of the flesh, the lust of the eyes*, and *the pride of life*, and none of these are of God. It's very likely that one or more of these allurements is what caused Demas to ditch his faith and return to Thessalonica. Let's take the remainder of this lesson to unpack the meaning of each of these classifications.

Number 1: Lust of the Flesh

The "lust of the flesh" is the first type of temptation John lists, and the Greek word for "lust" here is *epithumia*. It is from the word *epi*, which means *over* and gives intensity to the word; and the word *thumos*, which describes *passionate desire*. When these words are compounded to form *epithumia*, it describes *desire*, *cravings*, or *a longing*. A person given to "lust" (*epithumia*) is *one who is bent over longing and craving a thing*.

In this case, it is lust of the "flesh." In Greek, the word "flesh" is *sarkos*, and it describes *flesh*, *carnal nature*, or *base fleshly instincts*. This is a picture of *a hankering or obsession* for things of the flesh. The lust of the flesh is any temptation or sin that appeals to our carnal and physical appetites and seduces us away from our love for the Lord and our faith in Him.

Examples of the lust of the flesh include the works of the flesh, which Paul identifies in Galatians 5. These include drug addiction, alcoholism, gluttony, gossip, idolatry, materialism, physical violence, and fornication, which is all forms of sex outside the context of marriage between one man and one woman. (Rick meticulously unpacks what works of the flesh are and how to overcome them in his series *The Works of the Flesh vs. The Fruit of the Spirit*, which is available at **renner.org**.)

Number 2: Lust of the Eyes

The "lust of the eyes" is the second category of temptation offered by the world. For a second time, we see the word "lust" — the Greek word *epithumia*, from the words *epi* and *thumos*. The word *epi* means *over* and *gives intensity* to the word; the word *thumos* is *passionate desire*. When these words are compounded to form *epithumia*, it describes *desire*, *cravings*, or *a longing*. It is the picture of *one bent over and craving a thing*.

In this case, the hankering or intense craving is of the "eyes." In Greek, the word "eyes" is *opthalmos*, which describes *the eye*, but figuratively, it refers to *the mind's eye*. Please get this, because it is so important.

The eyes are a doorway to the mind, and whatever you continually look at — and ponder on — will eventually control you, and you'll become obsessed with it. Therefore, you must be very careful what you do with your eyes and what you allow them to view and stare at. If you're going to be pure — and remain pure — and walk in close companionship with the Lord, you must be intentional about guarding your eyes. Again, your eyes are a gate to your mind, and what you allow in will enter your mind.

This means you need to be intentional about...

- The **movies** you watch.

- The **books** and **magazines** you read.
- The **Internet websites** you visit.

The quality of the media you are consuming is the quality of life you will experience. If you're watching, listening to, and reading things that are violent, fearful, and filled with anger, hate, and negativity, you can expect your quality of life to reflect it. Likewise, if what you're taking in through your eyes is sensual, sexually stimulating, or morally debased, it is going to have a strong influence on every area of your life. Remember, "…For as he [a person] thinketh in his heart, so is he…" (Proverbs 23:7).

Again, the "lust of the eyes" specifically points to unhealthy, ungodly cravings generated by what we allow our eyes to see, which ultimately is *our mind's eye.* This also includes how we look at others sexually, so be careful how you view others. The lust of the eyes can also refer to the desire to want to have the things we see — like money, material possessions, houses, cars, or even a certain physical appearance. Our eyes see everything physical around us and can cause us to covet or want something we do not possess. Although there's nothing wrong with appreciating and wanting to have nice things, if your wants turn into *craving* and *coveting* things, the lust of the eyes is at work.

God has provided us with many powerful passages in His Word to help us protect our eyes, such as:

> **Psalm 101:3** — "I will set no wicked thing before mine eyes: I hate the work of them that turn aside; it shall not cleave to me."

> **Proverbs 28:16** (*NKJV*) — "…He who hates covetousness will prolong his days."

> **Luke 12:15** (*NKJV*) — "…Take heed and beware of covetousness, for one's life does not consist in the abundance of the things he possesses."

> **Psalm 119:37** (*NIV*) — "Turn my eyes away from worthless things; preserve my life according to your word."

Verses like these can and should become our declaration of faith. Nothing — absolutely no thing — is worth jeopardizing our walk with God. All of what we see is passing away, but our relationship with Him is forever.

Number 3: The Pride of Life

The third classification of temptation offered by the world is the "pride of life." The word "pride" in Greek is *aladzon*, and it describes *one full of himself, who goes about speaking about how great he is as he tries to be or to look outwardly impressive.* It is *one who is obsessed with self-importance.*

When we talk about the pride of life, we are talking about the following:

- A desire for power, personal recognition, and personal glory.
- A craving for influence or to be well thought of by others.
- A hankering and seeking after popularity and admiration at any cost.
- A craving for honor and applause.

The "pride of life" appeals to conceitedness, narcissism, and self-exaltation. It causes a person to believe he or she is better, more important than, or superior to others — usually based on his or her acquired material possessions, social status, education, and so on. The "pride of life" is a craving and yearning to be recognized, accepted, or applauded by others.

Knowing how fleeting and temporary this world is, the apostle John reminded us, "And the world passeth away, and the lust thereof: but he that doeth the will of God abideth for ever" (1 John 2:17). So not only are the things of this world temporary, but so is the craving and longing for what the world offers.

This means that even if we attempt to fulfill the lust of the flesh, the lust of the eyes, and the pride of life, that gratification won't last. Like everything else in the world, the fulfillment of these things is also temporary and passing away. It's only when we do the will of the Father that we experience eternal, lasting fulfillment and satisfaction.

No One's Exempt

Maybe you've read through this lesson and thought to yourself, *Well, I would never give place to the lust of the flesh, the lust of the eyes, and the pride of life!* If an idea like that went through your mind, consider the Holy Spirit's words through the apostle Paul in First Corinthians 10:12 (*NKJV*):

Therefore let him who thinks he stands take heed lest he fall.

The word "thinks" in this verse indicates having an opinion about one's own ability, which may or may not be based in reality. We can think that we are "better than that" — and that we would never fall for any of the temptations the world is offering. But this kind of thinking reeks of pride, hence the warning to not think we've got it all together and can never fall.

Taking into account the original Greek meaning, here is the *Renner Interpretive Version* (*RIV*) of First Corinthians 10:12:

> **If anyone has the opinion of himself that he is standing strong and firm, he needs to be continually watchful and always on his guard lest he trip, stumble, and fall from his overconfident position and take a nosedive to a serious crash!**

Demas likely fell victim to one or more of these three categories of temptation: the lust of the flesh, the lust of the eyes, or the pride of life. As a result, he abandoned Paul and his faith in Christ and went back to Thessalonica where he could disappear and blend in with the lifestyle of the pagans. Friend, the temptations of this world are formidable forces, but when you submit yourself to God, He will empower you to resist them and not abandon the faith!

In our final lesson, we'll examine five concrete steps you can take to make sure *you* never become a Demas.

STUDY QUESTIONS

Study to shew thyself approved unto God, a workman that needeth not to be ashamed, rightly dividing the word of truth.
— 2 Timothy 2:15

1. When you read about the three main types of temptation, what modern-day version of each one comes to mind? Which category seems to grab your attention and try to pull you in most frequently? To help you boost your spiritual immune system in this area, search for some specific scriptures that deal with this issue that will strengthen your spirit and guard your soul.

2. Name the dominant type of temptation that Samson, Lucifer, and Achan each fell prey to (*see* Judges 16; Isaiah 14:12-20; Joshua 7). What do their stories show you about the ways Satan works?

3. Proverbs 5:8 (*AMPC*) says, "Let your way in life be far from her [temptation], and come not near the door of her house [avoid the very scenes of temptation]." In what practical ways can you avoid the scenes of temptation in your life?

PRACTICAL APPLICATION

But be ye doers of the word, and not hearers only,
deceiving your own selves.
— James 1:22

1. To help you guard against the "lust of the eyes," the "lust of the flesh," and the "pride of life," take an honest inventory of the information and entertainment you are consuming. How does your media menu stack up to God's standards? Ask yourself:

   • The **movies** I'm watching…would I watch them with Jesus?

   • The **books** and **magazines** I'm reading… would I read them with Jesus?

   • The **Internet sites** I'm visiting…would I go there and look at them with Jesus?

   • The **music** I'm listening to…would Jesus listen to it and sing along?

   If you're having second thoughts — or are embarrassed — to think about Jesus looking at and listening to your media choices, invite the Holy Spirit to help you make some changes.

2. The next time you're getting ready to do a search or look up something or someone on the Internet, pause and imagine Jesus sitting right next to you. Imagine yourself handing Him your phone, your remote, or your mouse. Would you ask Him to type in and search for what you're about to look for? If not, ask Him to show you the need or desire behind that choice, to help you trust Him, and to show you how you can get your needs met in a healthy, godly way. Write out anything He shows you about the type of temptation you're more likely to struggle with.

3. What books, magazines, movies, and music choices do you know in your heart need to be deleted from your diet? What are some healthier media options that you can reach for instead? Pray and ask the Holy Spirit to direct you to more life-giving media choices (*see* Psalm 25:12).

(**NOTE**: It may be helpful for you to consider setting a guard on your phone, TV, computers, and other devices to help block damaging content such as pornography, violent video games, gambling sites, etc.)

TOPIC
Concrete Steps To Be Sure You Never Become a Demas

SCRIPTURES

1. **2 Timothy 4:9,10** — Do thy diligence to come shortly unto me: For Demas hath forsaken me, having loved this present world, and is departed unto Thessalonica....

2. **1 Corinthians 10:13** (*NKJV*) — No temptation has overtaken you except such as is common to man; but God is faithful, who will not allow you to be tempted beyond what you are able, but with the temptation will also make the way of escape, that you may be able to bear it.

3. **Proverbs 1:5** — A wise man will hear, and will increase learning; and a man of understanding shall attain unto wise counsels.

4. **Proverbs 19:27** — Cease, my son, to hear the instruction that causeth to err from the words of knowledge.

5. **Romans 10:17** — So then faith cometh by hearing, and hearing by the word of God.

6. **1 Timothy 4:1** — Now the Spirit speaketh expressly, that in the latter times some shall depart from the faith, giving heed to seducing spirits, and doctrines of devils.

7. **1 Timothy 4:6** — ...Nourished up in the words of faith and of good doctrine....

8. **2 Timothy 3:5,6** — Having a form of godliness, but denying the power thereof: from such turn away. For of this sort are they which creep into houses....

9. **Psalm 1:1** — Blessed is the man that walketh not in the counsel of the ungodly, nor standeth in the way of sinners, nor sitteth in the seat of the scornful.

10. **Psalm 26:4,5** — I have not sat with vain persons, neither will I go in with dissemblers. I have hated the congregation of evil doers; and will not sit with the wicked.

11. **Psalm 26:4,5** (*NASB*) — I do not sit with deceitful people, nor will I go with pretenders. I hate the assembly of evildoers, and I will not sit with the wicked.

12. **Proverbs 12:26** — The righteous is more excellent than his neighbour: but the way of the wicked seduceth them.

13. **Proverbs 18:24** (*NLT*) — There are "friends" who destroy each other, but a real friend sticks closer than a brother.

14. **Proverbs 22:24,25** — Make no friendship with an angry man; and with a furious man thou shalt not go: lest thou learn his ways, and get a snare to thy soul.

15. **1 Corinthians 5:11** — But now I have written unto you not to keep company, if any man that is called a brother be a fornicator, or covetous, or an idolater, or a railer, or a drunkard, or an extortioner; with such an one no not to eat.

16. **1 Corinthians 15:33** — Be not deceived: evil communications corrupt good manners.

17. **1 Corinthians 15:33** (*NASB*) — Do not be deceived: "Bad company corrupts good morals."

18. **2 Thessalonians 3:6** — Now we command you, brethren, in the name of our Lord Jesus Christ, that ye withdraw yourselves from every brother that walketh disorderly, and not after the tradition which he received of us.

19. **Galatians 6:10** — As we have therefore opportunity, let us do good unto all men, especially unto them who are of the household of faith.

20. **1 Timothy 3:15** — ...the house of God, which is the church of the living God, the pillar and ground of the truth.

21. **2 Peter 1:1** — ...them that have obtained like precious faith....

22. **2 Timothy 3:5** — Having a form of godliness, but denying the power thereof: from such turn away.

23. **Romans 12:1** — I beseech you therefore, brethren, by the mercies of God, that ye present your bodies a living sacrifice, holy, acceptable unto God, which is your reasonable service.

24. **Matthew 10:38** — And he that taketh not his cross, and followeth after me, is not worthy of me.

25. **Matthew 6:10** — Thy kingdom come, Thy will be done in earth, as it is in heaven.

26. **2 Peter 3:11** — Seeing then that all these things shall be dissolved, what manner of persons ought ye to be in all holy conversation and godliness.

27. **1 John 2:17** — And the world passeth away, and the lust thereof: but he that doeth the will of God abideth for ever.

28. **2 Corinthians 4:18** — While we look not at the things which are seen, but at the things which are not seen: for the things which are seen are temporal; but the things which are not seen are eternal.

29. **2 Corinthians 5:10** — For we must all appear before the Judgment Seat of Christ; that every one may receive the things done in his body, according to that he hath done, whether it be good or bad.

GREEK WORDS

1. "diligence" — **σπουδάζω** (*spoudadzo*): to do something with haste because it is so important, serious, or urgent; to give one's best efforts to a project or task and to do it enthusiastically

2. "shortly" — **ταχέως** (*tacheos*): from **ταχύς** (*tachus*); depicts a runner who runs as fast as he can; to move one's feet as fast as possible; to do something urgently; to do something as swiftly as possible

3. "for" — **γάρ** (*gar*): for because; for indeed; for verily; possibly carries an element of shock and surprise

4. "Demas" — **Δημᾶς** (*Demas*): a companion and helper of the apostle Paul; here, spoken of with commendation as one in whom the apostle had confidence; some scholars believe that Demas was the one who actually penned the book of Colossians as it was dictated by Paul; he was likely from aristocracy, privilege, and wealth

5. "forsaken" — **ἐγκαταλείπω** (*enkataleipo*): a compound of the prepositions ἐν (*en*) and **κατά** (*kata*), and the word λείπω (*leipo*); the preposition ἐν (*en*) means in, **κατά** (*kata*) means down, and the word λείπω (*leipo*) means to abandon, forsake, or leave behind; as a compound, to

abandon, forsake, or leave in a bad situation; not only to desert, but to do it in the worst way and at the worst possible moment; not merely to leave, but to leave in the lurch

6. "departed" — πορεύομαι (*poreuomai*): here, pictures one who has departed or transitioned from a former position to another; the implication is Demas did not begin in a wrong place, but for some reason, he abandoned his former place or position to follow after a new place or position that was very different

7. "common to man" — ἀνθρώπινος (*anthropinos*): commonplace to humans; a common human dilemma, problem, or trial that has already been faced and overcome by others in the past

8. "escape" — ἔκβασις (*ekbasis*): a compound of ἐκ (*ek*), which means out or to make an exit, and βάσις (*basis*), which means to step; as a compound, it means to walk out, as to walk out of a difficult place; to step out; to walk out of a trap; the act of removing oneself from a place that isn't good for you; to walk out of or away from

SYNOPSIS

It's safe to say that no one who sincerely gives his life to Jesus ever plans — or wants — to abandon Him and return to his previous way of living. When our hearts are awakened to the reality and intensity of His love, we want to serve Him wholeheartedly all the days of our life. One of the ways we achieve this goal is living a life of *daily surrender.* The apostle Paul said:

> **So here's what I want you to do, God helping you: Take your everyday, ordinary life — your sleeping, eating, going-to-work, and walking-around life — and place it before God as an offering....**
> **— Romans 12:1 (*MSG*)**

Surrendering our life to God daily is an act of humility and trust in His ability to keep us, shape us, direct us, and correct us so that at the end of the journey, we can hear the words we long to hear: "Well done, good and faithful servant! Enter into the joy of your Lord!" (*see* Matthew 25:23). In this final lesson, we will explore five biblical steps we can take to make sure we *never* become a Demas.

The emphasis of this lesson:

To avoid being a modern-day Demas: (1) Listen to and read right information; (2) choose the right friends; (3) go to the right church; (4) live every day at the altar of surrender; (5) never forget that eternity is before you.

A Final Review of Our Anchor Verse

In all our lessons, we have talked about a man named Demas who is mentioned three times in the New Testament. Paul noted him in his letters to the Colossian believers as well as to Philemon, including his name among other notable First Century Christian leaders like Epaphras, Mark, Luke, and Aristarchus. Demas served as a traveling companion and an assistant to Paul and was *deeply cherished, admired,* and *celebrated.*

But at some point, his heart changed, and he abandoned Paul, which is what we read about in Paul's second letter to Timothy. Paul said, "For Demas hath forsaken me, having loved this present world, and is departed unto Thessalonica..." (2 Timothy 4:10). The word "for" here carries the idea of *shock* and *surprise.* Paul was absolutely stunned that Demas had forsaken him. This was the same Demas who had been Paul's co-laborer and had likely written the book of Colossians as Paul dictated it.

Astonished and bewildered, Paul informed Timothy that Demas had "forsaken" him. We saw that the word "forsaken" is a translation of the Greek word *enkataleipo,* which means *to abandon, forsake,* or *leave in a bad situation.* Not only does it mean to desert, but to do it in the worst way and at the worst time possible. Rather than to merely leave, this word means *to leave someone in the lurch,* which is what Demas did to Paul.

Apparently, Demas had an unhealthy love and infatuation with the "present world." This means he had a misdirected affection for and attraction to *this present age* or *the here and now in this world.* As a result, the Bible says Demas "departed to Thessalonica" (2 Timothy 4:10). That word "departed" is the Greek word *poreuomai,* which pictures *one who has departed or transitioned from a former position to another.* That is most often what happens — people gradually walk away from their devotion to the Lord. The use of the word *poreuomai* indicates that Demas didn't begin in the wrong place, but for some reason, he abandoned his former place or position to follow a new place or position that was very different. This gradual departure from the faith is what the Bible calls *apostasy,* and it is taking place all around us just as the Holy Spirit predicted (*see* 1 Timothy 4:1).

There Is a Way of Escape!

It may be that right now you're being tempted to draw back from the Lord and modify or downplay your stance on biblical principles and standards that you once held to tightly. The good news is, you don't have to give in to that temptation — there is a way out! The Bible says, "No temptation has overtaken you except such as is common to man; but God is faithful, who will not allow you to be tempted beyond what you are able, but with the temptation will also make the way of escape, that you may be able to bear it" (1 Corinthians 10:13 *NKJV*).

Notice the words "common to man." These are a translation of the Greek word *anthropinos*, and it means *commonplace to humans*. It describes *a common human dilemma, problem, or trial that has already been faced and overcome by others in the past.* The fact that every temptation we face has been faced by someone else tells us we're not alone in the problems we're dealing with. If others have confronted and conquered, so can we.

Scripture says, "...But God is faithful, who will not allow you to be tempted beyond what you are able, but with the temptation will also make the way of escape, that you may be able to bear it" (1 Corinthians 10:13 *NKJV*). The word "escape" here is the Greek word *ekbasis*, a compound of *ek*, which means *out* or *to make an exit*, and *basis*, which means *to step*. When these words are joined, they make the word *ekbasis*, which means *to walk out*, as *to walk out of a difficult place*. It can also mean *to step out or to walk out of a trap*. It is *the act of removing oneself from a place that isn't good for you; to walk out of or away from.*

So when the Bible says God will make a way for you to *escape*, it means the answer is right under you — your feet! You'd be amazed at how many times the way of escape from what you're dealing with is simply to get up and walk away from where you are. Additionally, there are five concrete steps you can take to guard yourself from becoming a Demas.

Step 1: Listen To and Read Right Information

There's an old adage that says, "Garbage in, garbage out," and it is so true. Just as you are what you eat physically, you are what you eat spiritually. Everything you take in through your eyes and ears influences every aspect of your life. A steady diet of negative, fearful, and evil things is going to produce the same kinds of things in your life. Hence, you need to **listen to**

and read the right information. Consider what God's Word says in these verses:

Proverbs 1:5 says, "A wise man will hear, and will increase learning; and a man of understanding shall attain unto wise counsels."

Proverbs 19:27 says, "Cease, my son, to hear the instruction that causeth to err from the words of knowledge."

If you're listening to or looking at something that's causing you to *err* from the faith you've been rooted in, you need to discard it and replace it with things that will help you stay strong in your faith. So many people today — especially our young people — are being lured away and deceived by what they're hearing on the Internet, from friends, or from university professors. As you might have heard it said before, *don't be so open-minded that your brain falls out.* Instead, stay rooted in the unchanging, essential doctrines of Scripture that you've been taught. The Bible says:

So then faith cometh by hearing, and hearing by the word of God.
— Romans 10:17

Are you hearing words of doubt and fear? Or are you hearing words of faith? What you feed will grow. What you starve will die. If you're listening to negativism, it will produce a negative, defeated life. If you want to be strong in your faith in Christ, continue listening to things that produce faith.

In First Timothy 4:1, Paul prophesied, saying, "Now the Spirit speaketh expressly, that in the latter times some shall depart from the faith, giving heed to seducing spirits, and doctrines of devils." The reason some are departing from the faith is, they're listening to and watching the wrong things. Friend, if the news and entertainment you're feeding on is stirring up fear, anger, and unbelief regarding the things of God, turn it off and find something else that is both true and life-giving. Indeed, you are to be "...nourished up in the words of faith and of good doctrine..." (1 Timothy 4:6).

So many people in the world today fit the description of Second Timothy 3:5, which says, "Having a form of godliness, but denying the power thereof...." The verse goes on to say, "...From such turn away." In these last of the last days, the Bible warns, "For of this sort are they which creep into houses..." (2 Timothy 3:6). You need to be careful about what you allow to "creep into your house" through your devices. Just because it looks good and you can watch it doesn't mean you should. Your life — and the lives of your loved ones — are precious. So be careful what you're listening to and make sure you're reading and watching the right information.

Step 2: Choose the Right Friends

Do you want to have a good idea of what your future will be like? Look at the caliber of people you're hanging out with on a regular basis. **Choosing the right friends** is vital to you keeping your faith. Unhealthy friends will lead you astray; healthy, godly friends will preserve your way. Psalm 1:1 says, "Blessed is the man that walketh not in the counsel of the ungodly, nor standeth in the way of sinners, nor sitteth in the seat of the scornful." Our life is blessed when we are not closely connected with ungodly, scornful people.

When it came to being in close relationship with evildoers, David said:

> **I have not sat with vain persons, neither will I go in with dissemblers. I have hated the congregation of evil doers; and will not sit with the wicked.**
> **— Psalm 26:4,5**

Here is this same passage in the *New American Standard Bible*:

> **I do not sit with deceitful people, nor will I go with pretenders. I hate the assembly of evildoers, and I will not sit with the wicked.**
> **— Psalm 26:4,5 (*NASB*)**

Here we see David unashamedly make a solid decision to not keep company with evildoers, pretenders, or deceitful people. He knew how subtle and seductive their influence could be on his life. We see this sentiment echoed in his son Solomon's words:

> **The righteous is more excellent than his neighbour: but the way of the wicked seduceth them.**
> **— Proverbs 12:26**

You need to be careful not to be seduced in the wrong direction by those who claim to be your friends. When you enter a friendship with someone, you are giving that person a "seat" at the table in your life. Since there are only a few seats that are close to you, be careful about who you give them to. This next verse expands on this principle stating:

> **There are "friends" who destroy each other, but a real friend sticks closer than a brother.**
> — **Proverbs 18:24 (*NLT*)**

Indeed, there are some people who will bring out the absolute worst in you and others who will bring out the best. It's your job to choose friends who motivate you to draw closer to God and do right. When you do, you won't go wrong.

What else does the Bible tell us about friendships?

> **Make no friendship with an angry man; and with a furious man thou shalt not go: lest thou learn his ways, and get a snare to thy soul.**
> — **Proverbs 22:24,25**

> **But now I have written unto you not to keep company, if any man that is called a brother be a fornicator, or covetous, or an idolater, or a railer, or a drunkard, or an extortioner; with such an one no not to eat.**
> — **1 Corinthians 5:11**

These passages are all about influence. If you develop a friendship with someone who is angry and filled with strife, you will unconsciously begin to mimic his or her ways, and it will be a trap to you. Likewise, if you hang around those who call themselves Christians and are involved in sexual sin, idolatry, drunkenness, or cheating others, your character will be tainted by theirs. It won't be long before they tempt you (whether on purpose or by default) and even expect you to fall in line and do the same things. Avoid becoming close friends with these kinds of people at all costs — choose to pray for them, but don't give them a seat of influence at your table. First Corinthians 15:33 says:

> **Be not deceived: evil communications corrupt good manners.**

This same verse in the *New American Standard Bible* says:

> **Do not be deceived: "Bad company corrupts good morals."**

Last, but certainly not least, Second Thessalonians 3:6 tells us, "Now we command you, brethren, in the name of our Lord Jesus Christ, that ye withdraw yourselves from every brother that walketh disorderly, and not after the tradition which he received of us." Clearly, if you choose the wrong friends, your life will suffer for it. But when you choose the right friends, your life will be blessed.

Step 3: Go to the Right Church

The Bible clearly states, "We should not stop gathering together with other believers, as some of you are doing. Instead, we must continue to encourage each other even more as we see the day of the Lord coming" (Hebrews 10:25 *GW*). Friend, *going to the right church* is one of the best things you can do to keep yourself from becoming a Demas. In a healthy church, we help and watch out for one other. Galatians 6:10 says:

> **As we have therefore opportunity, let us do good unto all men, especially unto them who are of the household of faith.**

Are you going to a church that produces *faith* in your heart? Or are you hearing preaching and teaching that produces doubt and unbelief? Are you hearing messages that motivate you to trust the integrity of God's Word or doubt it? You need to go to a place that is a household of *faith*.

According to First Timothy 3:15, "…The house of God, which is the church of the living God, [is] the pillar and ground of the truth." Friend, you need to be going to a church that upholds the Word of God — and doesn't add or take away from it. Likewise, you need to be fellowshipping with "…them that have obtained like precious faith…" (2 Peter 1:1). In other words, make sure you're attending a church where the pastor and the people have a faith that is similar to yours.

A HEALTHY CHURCH:

- Treasures and teaches God's Word accurately to equip the saints for the work of service.
- Proclaims the Gospel without compromise.
- Makes disciples who live in the power of the Holy Spirit.
- Undergirds everything in prayer.
- Emphasizes reaching the lost (both locally and globally).
- Has leaders who are mature and godly and who walk in integrity.
- Deals lovingly and biblically with sinning members.

- Has leadership who is in relationship with other mature, godly leaders who walk in integrity and can help provide support and accountability.

Remember, the Holy Spirit prophesied through Paul that in the last days, there will be people "having a form of Godliness, but denying the power thereof . . . (2 Timothy 3:5). The rest of that verse says, ". . . From such turn away." In Greek, "turn away" means *to put space between yourself and them*. This means, if you're going to a church that denies the operation of the Holy Spirit or denies the immutability (unchanging nature) of God's Word, you need to put space between yourself and that church and get out of there.

Take a moment and ask yourself this question: "If I keep myself and my family in the spiritual environment we are in at the present time, what kind of harvest will it produce in us in the future?" In other words, "Am I going to a church or denomination that fosters love for the Bible, faith in the infallible Word of God, and belief in the operation of God's power?" Realize that everything is at stake when it comes to being in the right or wrong spiritual environment.

Step 4: Live Every Day at the Altar of Surrender

The fourth step to never becoming a Demas is to **live every day at the altar of surrender**. One of the best verses to communicate this truth is Romans 12:21, where the apostle Paul says:

> **I beseech you therefore, brethren, by the mercies of God, that ye present your bodies a living sacrifice, holy, acceptable unto God, which is your reasonable service.**

Along these same lines, Jesus said, "...Anyone who wants to follow me must put aside his own desires and conveniences and carry his cross with him every day and keep close to me" (Luke 9:23 *TLB*). Furthermore, in Matthew 10:38, He said, "And he that taketh not his cross, and followeth after me, is not worthy of me."

Jesus is not asking us to do anything that He Himself didn't do. Keep in mind, when He taught us how to pray, part of His model prayer was, "Thy kingdom come, Thy will be done in earth, as it is in heaven" (Matthew 6:10). To see the will of God in Heaven become the will of God on earth — especially in our lives — we have to live daily at the altar of surrender. That is, we must die to what *we want*, what *we think*, and how *we feel*, and live for what God knows is best for our lives.

Step 5: Never Forget Eternity Is Before You

The fifth step to avoiding the path of apostasy taken by Demas is to *never forget eternity is before you*. Look at what the apostle Peter wrote:

> **Seeing then that all these things shall be dissolved, what manner of persons ought ye to be in all holy conversation and godliness.**
> **— 2 Peter 3:11**

Everything that we see around us is in a state of decay and is going to pass away. The visible is temporary. It's the invisible — what we cannot see — that is eternal. The apostle John wrote:

> **And the world passeth away, and the lust thereof: but he that doeth the will of God abideth for ever.**
> **— 1 John 2:17**

Again, the world and all its systems of politics, fashion, entertainment, education, and government will all pass away. Therefore, we need to focus on doing the will of God, which includes the specific life-assignment(s) He's given to us.

The apostle Paul declared:

> **While we look not at the things which are seen, but at the things which are not seen: for the things which are seen are temporal; but the things which are not seen are eternal.**
> **— 2 Corinthians 4:18**

This passage is a good reminder of what we learned in Lesson 4, and that is to not allow ourselves to be mesmerized and lured away from God by *the lust of the eyes*. What our eyes see is temporary, but the things that are unseen are eternal. Hence, **living with eternity before you** will help you keep your eyes on the everlasting prize and avoid temptation. And by all means, never forget the sobering truth of Second Corinthians 5:10:

> **For we must all appear before the Judgment Seat of Christ; that every one may receive the things done in his body, according to that he hath done, whether it be good or bad.**

Hopefully, you are beginning to understand the importance of what you allow your eyes to see, who you choose as your friends, what church you go to, living a life of surrender every day, and never forgetting eternity is in front of you.

How do you think Demas' life would have turned out had he taken these steps? More than likely, he would not have abandoned Paul, his faith, or the Lord and become a pagan priest in the city of Thessalonica — he would have stayed strong and held on to his eternal reward instead of forfeiting it for temporary ease.

Friend, Demas' story of falling away does NOT have to be your story. If you'll continue to intentionally pursue closeness with Christ and heed the truths presented in this series — including the five steps in this final lesson — you can stay on track and choose a better ending for your story than Demas.'

STUDY QUESTIONS

Study to shew thyself approved unto God, a workman that needeth not to be ashamed, rightly dividing the word of truth.
— 2 Timothy 2:15

1. Can you think of anyone in the Bible who chose wrong friends, and it *didn't* affect him? How about in your own life? Is there anyone you know who hung around people who were a bad influence, and it *didn't* affect him or her negatively? What does this say to you?

2. Who in the Old Testament did NOT choose the right friends, and ended losing his entire kingdom? What happened? (*See* First Kings 12:1-24.)

3. Did you know that even people who seem to be solid believers and leaders can sometimes mislead others? Read the sobering story in First Kings 13 and write what stands out to you. Now go back and read Galatians 1:8-12. What is the connection between these two passages, and what do they show you about the importance of holding to the truth of Scripture and sticking with what God has revealed to you personally?

PRACTICAL APPLICATION

But be ye doers of the word, and not hearers only,
deceiving your own selves.
— James 1:22

1. What sources of information and/or media do you normally go
    to in order to stay up to date on what's going on in the world as a
    whole? Take a moment to measure them against the standard for our
    thoughts that God gives us in Philippians 4:8. Are they a good, godly
    fit? If not, which ones need to go?

2. How does remembering that *eternity is in front of you* — and that you will
    one day stand before God and give an account for what you did in this
    life — influence the way you live? As you answer this question, consider
    what God says in Romans 14:10-12; Matthew 16:27; 25:31-46;
    First Peter 1:17; Second Corinthians 5:9,10; and Revelation 22:12.
    What is the Holy Spirit revealing to you?

3. *Going to the right church* is one of the most important safeguards to
    keep you off the path of apostasy. Take a moment and honestly answer
    these questions:

    • Are you *regularly* attending a healthy church? Or is your attendance
    hit or miss?

    • How do you know the church you're going to is healthy? Of the
    eight signs of a healthy church presented in this lesson, which ones
    can you see operating in your church?

    • If you are going to the right church, how has being a part of the
    local body of believers strengthened you and even kept you from
    going in the wrong direction? Share any stories that come to mind.

4. Jesus said very clearly that if we want to be His disciple, we must
    surrender our life to Him daily, take up our "cross," and follow Him
    (*see* Matthew 16:24-26; Luke 9:23-25). Essentially, this is *living every
    day at the altar of surrender*. In your own words, describe how this might
    look in your life. (As you answer, consider what the Bible says in
    First Corinthians 10:24; Philippians 2:3,4; as well as in Romans 13:12-14;
    Colossians 3:1-9; First Peter 4:1,2; Galatians 5:16, 24.)

Notes

Notes

Notes

CLAIM YOUR FREE RESOURCE!

As a way of introducing you further to the teaching ministry of Rick Renner, we would like to send you FREE of charge his teaching, "How To Receive a Miraculous Touch From God" on CD or as an MP3 download.

In His earthly ministry, Jesus commonly healed *all* who were sick of *all* their diseases. In this profound message, learn about the manifold dimensions of Christ's wisdom, goodness, power, and love toward all humanity who came to Him in faith with their needs.

☑ **YES, I want to receive Rick Renner's monthly teaching letter!**

Simply scan the QR code to claim this resource or go to: **renner.org/claim-your-free-offer**

Connect

WITH US!

www.ingramcontent.com/pod-product-compliance
Lightning Source LLC
Chambersburg PA
CBHW071639040426
42452CB00009B/1701